Vintage Hustle

Building Booths that Last

By Rodney Baker

Copyright Page

For permission requests, write to the publisher at the address below:
Rustique Relics LLC
706 2nd Ave N
Clanton, AL 35045
Email: admin@rustiquerelics.com
First Edition: 2026
ISBN: 979-8-9989738-1-9
Printed in the United States of America
Cover and interior design by Rodney Baker

This book is a work of nonfiction. The information contained within is based on the author's personal experiences and insights. While every effort has been made to ensure accuracy, the author and publisher assume no responsibility for errors, omissions, or outcomes resulting from the use of this material.

Disclaimer

The information contained in this book is for general informational and educational purposes only. It is not intended as legal, financial, or professional advice. Readers are encouraged to consult appropriate professionals before making business decisions. The author and Rustique Relics LLC make no representations or warranties regarding the accuracy, applicability, or completeness of the contents. The reader assumes full responsibility for their use of the information contained herein. The author disclaims any liability for any damages or losses incurred by the reader in connection with the use of this book

Dedication

Because nothing is accomplished alone

I would like to start by thanking **God**, who gave purpose to the work long before I understood it.

For my wife **Missy**, my partner in every sense of the word. There's no telling what would have happened had I been left to my own devices.

For our **kids,** who grew up alongside this business and remind me what truly lasts.

For our **customers**, your continued support, kind words, and shared love for all things vintage are what keep this dream alive.

For our **vendors**, past, present, and future, who trusted us with their work and helped turn a building into a community.

And for our **readers**, the vendors who keep showing up, adjusting, and learning, this book exists because of you.

THANK YOU

Table of Contents

Introduction

Who This Book Is For—and Why It Exists

I would like to start this book off by saying, **this book was not written for beginners**.

It wasn't written for people chasing quick wins, side-hustle fantasies, or viral success.

It wasn't written for vendors who want a checklist they can follow for thirty days and call it a strategy.

This book is for vendors who already know how to sell—but don't always know *why* it still works... or why it sometimes doesn't.

It's for the vendor whose booth is technically fine, but emotionally exhausting.

For the one who restocks, rearranges, adjusts, and experiments—yet still feels like the booth requires constant attention just to stay upright.

For the vendor who remembers when things felt easier, faster, lighter—and can't quite explain what changed.

If you've ever thought:

- *"I shouldn't be struggling this much—I know how to do this."*
- *"Sales aren't terrible, but this doesn't feel sustainable."*
- *"I'm working harder than I should have to at this stage."*

This book was written for you.

Most vendor advice focuses on getting started. Very little addresses what happens *after* you've already built something. After you've proven you can sell. After the booth pays its rent. After momentum slows—not because you failed, but because the environment changed.

That middle stage is where most experienced vendors get stuck.

1

Not because they lack effort or creativity—but because the strategies that built early success don't always scale into stability. What once felt effective begins to feel fragile. Decisions take more energy. Small problems feel heavier than they should. And eventually, the booth stops feeling like an asset and starts feeling like a responsibility.

This book exists to explain *why* that happens—and how to fix it without starting over.

> It is not about hustling harder.
> It is not about chasing trends.
> It is not about doing more.

It's about learning how to **remove friction, protect systems**, and **build booths that hold together when life pulls your attention elsewhere**.

I've written this from both sides of the counter—as a vendor who has made the mistakes you're trying to avoid, and as a store owner who has watched hundreds of booths plateau, break through, overextend, and burn out. I've seen how often good vendors blame themselves for problems that are actually structural. And I've seen how quietly powerful it is when a booth finally becomes predictable, forgiving, and resilient.

That kind of success doesn't feel loud.

> It feels steady.
> It feels manageable.
> It feels like choice.

If you're looking for motivation, this may not be the book you want.

If you're looking for clarity, alignment, and a way to make your booth support your life instead of competing with it—

You're exactly where you're supposed to be.

Before we begin there are several concepts that will be repeated throughout, this is intentional. My hope is that this will help to show how each part of your booth is interconnected and hopefully unwind it so that building a booth that lasts is not as daunting a challenge as it may seem.

With all that out of the way—Let's Begin!

This Market Didn't Kill Your Booth

If you spend any time in antique and vintage social media groups right now, you'll see the same conversations repeating themselves like clockwork.

> Sales are down.
> Foot traffic feels lighter.
> People aren't buying like they used to.
> Someone is packing up their booth.
> Someone else is "taking a break."
> And more than a few are openly talking about quitting altogether.

The wording changes, but the conclusion rarely does.

> *The market is dead.*

That belief has become so common that many vendors accept it as fact without ever questioning it. And once you accept that conclusion, everything that follows feels inevitable. Declining sales feel unavoidable. Motivation drops. Effort becomes mechanical. Eventually, quitting starts to feel reasonable—even responsible.

Here's the truth most people don't want to hear, but desperately need to:

This market didn't kill your booth.
What it *did* do was change the rules.

And change is uncomfortable—especially when what you were doing used to work.

The Market Didn't Collapse — It Shifted

When vendors say the market is bad, what they usually mean is that the market no longer behaves the way it used to.

There *was* a time when:

- Almost anything vintage would sell eventually
- Full booths could coast on charm alone

- Pricing mistakes were forgiven
- Shoppers lingered longer
- Competition was thinner and less curated

That version of the market rewarded **presence** more than **precision**. If you showed up consistently with decent inventory, sales eventually followed.

Today's market doesn't reward that anymore.

> Modern shoppers are more selective.
> They're more informed.
> They're more distracted.
> And they're spending with intention—or not at all.

That doesn't mean people stopped buying vintage, antiques, or handmade items. It means they stopped buying *carelessly*.

This distinction matters more than most vendors realize.

> A market collapse eliminates demand.
> A market shift **changes how demand behaves**.

Vendors who recognized this early adjusted quietly. Vendors who didn't felt blindsided, frustrated, and confused—often without understanding why.

Why "It Feels Slower" Even When People Are Still Buying
One of the most disorienting parts of today's market is that it doesn't *look* dead.

Malls still have traffic.
Shoppers still browse.
People still pick things up, put them down, and walk away.

What's changed is *conversion*.

Shoppers are:

- More cautious
- More price-aware
- Less impulsive
- Faster to move on

They're comparing booths mentally instead of emotionally. They're scanning for value, story, and uniqueness instead of just charm.

This creates a dangerous illusion for vendors:

"If people are walking through, my booth should be selling."

But foot traffic alone is no longer enough. Visibility without intention no longer converts.

Why So Many Good Vendors Feel Like They're Failing

One of the hardest truths for established vendors to accept is this:

You can be doing nothing "wrong" and still be doing something that no longer works.

That's why this frustration feels personal.

> You didn't suddenly forget how to source.
> You didn't lose your eye.
> You didn't become lazy or careless.

In fact, many struggling vendors are working harder than they ever have. They're restocking more often. Rearranging constantly. Lowering prices. Running sales.

And none of it feels like it's helping.

That's because effort alone doesn't solve misalignment.

If your booth is built around yesterday's buying habits, it will struggle in today's market—no matter how good your inventory is.

This is where many vendors get stuck.

They assume:

- Struggling means they're failing
- Quitting is the logical next step
- Everyone else is doing just as badly

Most of the time, none of those assumptions are true.

The Emotional Cost of "Used to Work"

Established vendors carry something newer vendors don't: **memory**.

> You remember when items moved faster.
> You remember better months.
> You remember the excitement of consistent sales.

That memory can quietly become a liability.

Instead of asking *"What does this booth need now?"*, you start asking *"Why isn't this selling like it used to?"*

Those are very different questions.

One leads to adaptation.
The other leads to frustration.

And frustration, when left unchecked, turns into burnout.

Social Media Groups Are Loud — Not Accurate

Online vendor groups feel comforting because they validate how many people feel right now.

But validation is not the same thing as clarity.

> People who are doing well rarely post about it.
> People who are busy selling aren't debating the market.
> People who are adapting don't argue—they adjust.

What you see online is not a representative sample of all vendors. It's a concentration of stress, uncertainty, and fear bouncing between people who all feel stuck at the same time.

> That environment doesn't encourage perspective.
> It encourages agreement.

And agreement feels good—but it doesn't fix anything.

When enough people repeat the same belief, it starts to sound like truth. But repetition does not make a conclusion accurate.

Why Quitting Feels Like the Right Answer (Even When It Isn't)

When your booth stops performing the way it used to, the emotional toll builds slowly.

> You restock and nothing moves.
> You rearrange and sales stay flat.
> You lower prices and regret it.
> You raise prices and panic.

Eventually, curiosity is replaced by exhaustion.

Quitting stops feeling like failure and starts feeling like relief.

And in some cases, quitting *is* the right decision—but far less often than people think.

Most of the time, quitting doesn't mean the booth was doomed. It means the **strategy was never updated**.

I've watched too many solid vendors walk away—not because they couldn't succeed, but because no one helped them understand *why* things stopped working.

This Book Is Not About Blaming the Market

Markets change. They always have.

What separates vendors who survive from those who burn out isn't hustle—it's **adaptability**.

This book is not about:

- Grinding harder
- Buying more inventory
- Following trends blindly
- Pretending everything is fine

It *is* about:

- Understanding where friction is coming from
- Identifying blind spots you can't see from inside your own booth
- Making strategic adjustments instead of emotional ones

- Learning how to grind with purpose instead of panic

This is not a motivational book.
It's a **recalibration.**

A Necessary Reframe Before We Go Any Further

Before we talk about inventory, pricing, layout, or data, one thing has to be clear:

Struggling does not mean you're bad at this.

It means you're operating in a market that no longer rewards the same behavior it once did.

That's not a judgment.
It's a reality.

And reality is workable—once you understand it.

But only if you're willing to stop asking:

"Why is this market so bad?"

And start asking:

"What is this market responding to now?"

That question changes everything.

Chapter Takeaway

The market didn't end your booth—it exposed the limits of a strategy that used to work. The vendors who succeed next aren't the ones who complain the loudest; they're the ones who adapt first.

Looking Ahead

In the next chapter, we'll tackle one of the most dangerous traps for experienced vendors: emotional attachment to past success—and why *"it used to sell better"* can quietly sabotage everything you do next.

The Myth of "It Used to Sell Better"

Few phrases are as common—or as quietly destructive—in the antique and vintage world as this one:

"It used to sell better."

Most vendors say it casually. Almost reflexively. As if it's an observation rather than a belief. But that phrase carries weight, and the longer it goes unchallenged, the more damage it does to decision-making, confidence, and momentum.

Because "it used to sell better" is rarely just a statement of fact.

More often, it's a justification.

When Memory Becomes the Measuring Stick

Established vendors rely heavily on memory. That's not a flaw—it's experience. You remember what moved quickly. You remember which categories paid your rent. You remember the items that couldn't stay on the shelf.

Those memories helped you build your booth in the first place.

But memory is not neutral.

> Memory smooths over slow periods.
> Memory exaggerates peak moments.
> Memory forgets context.

What you remember as "consistent sales" may have actually been seasonal spikes. What you remember as "fast movers" may have been popular because they were uncommon *at the time*. And what you remember as "working" may have been supported by a market environment that no longer exists.

When memory becomes the primary measuring stick, the present will always feel like a disappointment.

The Subtle Shift From Observation to Attachment

There's nothing wrong with noticing a change. The problem starts when noticing turns into clinging.

At first, "it used to sell better" sounds reasonable. It feels analytical. But over time, it becomes emotionally loaded. You stop asking why something isn't moving and start defending it instead.

> You give items more time than they deserve.
> You avoid repricing because "someone will come along."
> You rearrange instead of reevaluating.

Eventually, you're no longer managing inventory—you're protecting history.

That's when progress stalls.

Yesterday's Winners Can Quietly Sabotage Today's Booth

One of the hardest realities for experienced vendors is this:

Past success does not guarantee present relevance.

In fact, past success can make adaptation harder.

When an item category or style carried your booth for years, it earns a kind of immunity in your mind. You trust it. You give it more space. You assume it will come back around.

But the market doesn't reward loyalty to inventory. It rewards relevance.

Customers don't know—or care—that something sold well five years ago. They only know whether it speaks to them *now*.

If it doesn't, nostalgia won't save it.

The Emotional Cost of Waiting for the Market to "Come Back"

Many vendors aren't refusing to adapt. They're waiting.

Waiting for the economy to improve.
Waiting for foot traffic to increase.
Waiting for buyers to behave the way they used to.

Waiting feels safe because it avoids hard decisions.

But waiting has a cost.

While you wait:

- Capital stays tied up in stagnant inventory
- Space remains underproductive
- Confidence erodes quietly
- Frustration compounds

Waiting isn't neutral. It's a choice—and often an expensive one.

Markets don't "come back" the way people expect. They evolve forward, not backward.

Why "But Everyone Used to Buy This" Doesn't Matter

This is one of the most common defenses vendors make when something stops selling.

And it's understandable.

If something worked across multiple years, multiple seasons, and multiple layouts, it *feels* dependable. But dependability is contextual.

Shoppers today:

- Compare more
- Buy fewer items per visit
- Spend more time browsing and less time committing
- Are more influenced by presentation than category

What once sold because it was available now has to sell because it stands out.

Availability is no longer a competitive advantage.

When Familiar Inventory Becomes Invisible

There's another layer to this myth that vendors rarely consider: **customer blindness**.

Regular shoppers don't see your booth the way you do. They see it as a mental snapshot. If that snapshot doesn't change meaningfully, their brain filters it out.

Inventory that once excited regular customers becomes background noise—not because it's bad, but because it's familiar.

That's why "but it's good stuff" isn't enough anymore.

Good, familiar, and unchanged is invisible.

The Comfort Trap of Emotional Pricing

Pricing is where "it used to sell better" does the most damage.

Vendors hesitate to reprice items downward because they remember what they *used* to get for them. They hesitate to reprice upward because they fear driving customers away.

So prices freeze.

Frozen prices lead to frozen inventory.

And frozen inventory quietly kills booth momentum.

Pricing should respond to reality, not memory. When it doesn't, inventory becomes a museum instead of a marketplace.

Letting Data Replace Memory

The antidote to this myth isn't pessimism—it's clarity.

Instead of asking:

- "Why isn't this selling like it used to?"

Ask:

- "How long has this been here?"

- "How much space is it consuming?"
- "What is it preventing me from bringing in?"
- "If I saw this for the first time today, would I buy it?"

These questions remove emotion from the equation and replace it with usefulness.

Data doesn't care about nostalgia. It cares about performance.

Relevance Is Not Betrayal

Many vendors feel like moving away from past success is a betrayal of their identity. Like they're abandoning what made them "them."

That belief is unnecessary—and harmful.

Adapting doesn't mean erasing your style.
It means refining it.

>It means curating instead of repeating.
>It means editing instead of accumulating.

Your booth can still reflect you without being stuck in time.

The Difference Between Honoring the Past and Living in It

Honoring the past means learning from it.

Living in it means refusing to move forward.

Every successful vendor eventually has to choose which one they're doing.

The market doesn't punish experience.
It punishes rigidity.

A Necessary Shift Before We Go Further

Before we talk about layout, inventory density, or category pivots, one thing has to happen:

You have to release the idea that past performance is owed a future return.

Nothing is guaranteed.

And that's not discouraging—it's freeing.

Once you stop waiting for the market to behave like it used to, you can start building a booth that works *now*.

Chapter Takeaway

"It used to sell better" is not a strategy—it's a memory. The vendors who succeed next aren't the ones protecting the past; they're the ones willing to re-evaluate it honestly.

Looking Ahead

In the next chapter, we'll address one of the loudest—and most misleading—sources of vendor frustration today: why social media groups feel like market truth, and how they quietly distort decision-making.

Why Social Groups Feel Like Market Truth and Why They're Not

If you spend any amount of time in antique or vintage social media groups, it's easy to come away with one overwhelming conclusion:

"This market is dead."

The posts sound confident. The comments pile on. The agreement feels unanimous. When dozens—or hundreds—of vendors echo the same frustration, it stops feeling like opinion and starts feeling like evidence.

But that feeling is deceptive.

Social media groups don't reflect the market. They reflect emotion. And when emotion becomes the primary source of feedback, decision-making quietly breaks down.

This chapter isn't about criticizing online communities. Social media groups can be useful. They can be encouraging. They can help vendors feel less alone.

But they are terrible at telling the truth about what's actually happening in the market.

And confusing emotional consensus with market reality is one of the fastest ways to stall your booth.

The Illusion of Consensus

Human brains are wired to trust patterns. When we see the same complaint repeated often enough, we assume it must be accurate.

If fifty vendors say sales are down, it feels irresponsible not to believe them.

But volume does not equal accuracy.

Social media creates the illusion of consensus because it concentrates similar voices in one place. When a post gains traction, it's not because it's true—it's because it's relatable. And relatability spreads faster than nuance.

A vendor posts:
"Anyone else struggling this month?"

Ten people respond:
"Same here."
"It's awful."
"This market is terrible."

Now it feels confirmed.

But what's missing from that thread is just as important as what's present.

You're not seeing:

- Vendors who had a strong month
- Vendors who adjusted and recovered
- Vendors who quietly reworked their booths and moved forward

Not because they don't exist—but because they aren't posting.

Consensus feels real because dissent is silent.

Why Struggling Vendors Are the Loudest Voices
People don't post when things are working. They post when something feels wrong.

Struggling vendors are seeking reassurance, not analysis. They want to know they aren't alone. And there's nothing wrong with that—until reassurance replaces responsibility.

Successful vendors tend to:

- Be busy sourcing
- Be busy restocking
- Be busy experimenting
- Be busy selling

They're not scrolling for validation. They're not narrating their wins. In many cases, they intentionally stay quiet because posting success invites criticism, jealousy, or unwanted advice.

So the loudest voices in groups skew negative—not because the market is universally bad, but because frustration is more likely to be shared than stability.

That creates a distorted sample.

You're not hearing from "the market."
You're hearing from "the frustrated portion of the market."

Those are not the same thing.

How Group Complaints Become Self-Reinforcing
Once a narrative takes hold in a group, it feeds itself.

> Someone blames the economy.
> Someone blames younger shoppers.
> Someone blames resellers.
> Someone blames landlords.
> Someone blames social media algorithms.

Each explanation reduces personal accountability just a little more.

Over time, the conversation shifts from:
"What can I change?"
to
"This is out of my control."

That shift feels comforting—but it's dangerous.

Because once responsibility dissolves into shared frustration, effort follows it out the door.

This is where Chapter 2 and Chapter 3 intersect.

> Memory becomes belief.
> Belief becomes permission.
> Permission becomes stagnation.

When groups normalize stagnation, doing nothing starts to feel reasonable.

The Dangerous Shift From Learning to Coping

At their best, vendor groups are educational.
At their worst, they become coping mechanisms.

There's a subtle but important difference.

Learning groups ask:

- What worked?
- What didn't?
- Why?
- What did you change?

Coping groups ask:

- Anyone else struggling?
- Is it just me?
- This market is terrible, right?

One leads to adjustment.
The other leads to emotional relief without improvement.

And emotional relief can be addictive.

If every time you feel discouraged, you can open an app and find instant validation, there's very little incentive to do the uncomfortable work of reevaluation.

Support is healthy.
Stagnation disguised as solidarity is not.

Why "Everyone Is Struggling" Is a Comfort Lie

One of the most repeated phrases in online vendor spaces is:
"Everyone is struggling right now."

It feels empathetic.
It feels fair.
It feels unifying.

But it's rarely true.

> Some vendors are struggling.
> Some vendors are stable.
> Some vendors are quietly thriving.

Lumping all outcomes together erases the most important variable: decision-making.

If everyone is struggling equally, then effort doesn't matter.
If effort doesn't matter, then adjustment feels pointless.
If adjustment feels pointless, nothing changes.

That's not reality—that's resignation.

Markets don't flatten performance. They amplify differences.

The gap between vendors who adapt and vendors who don't widens quietly, not loudly.

The Problem with Borrowed Confidence

Another subtle danger of group consensus is borrowed confidence.

When a group agrees that something "should" sell, vendors feel justified holding onto it—even when evidence says otherwise.

You see phrases like:

- "Those always sell."
- "People just aren't buying like they used to."
- "I'm not lowering my prices."

These statements feel strong. They sound decisive. But often they're borrowed—not earned.

Confidence that isn't backed by performance is fragile. And fragile confidence collapses the moment it's tested.

Real confidence comes from:

- Watching items move
- Seeing adjustments work
- Measuring results over time

Anything else is noise.

Why Groups Are Terrible at Diagnosing Booth Problems
Social media groups are general by nature.
Booths are specific by nature.

A group can't see:

- Your layout
- Your density
- Your pricing structure
- Your restock habits
- Your category balance
- Your booth's location within a mall

Yet advice is often given as if those details don't matter.

They matter immensely.

What works in one booth may fail in another—not because the market is broken, but because context is everything.

General advice applied to specific problems often makes things worse.

How to Use Social Media Groups without Letting Them Use You
This isn't a call to leave groups. It's a call to use them intentionally.

Groups are useful for:

- Trend awareness (not trend adoption)
- Vendor logistics
- Supplier recommendations
- Emotional perspective, in moderation

Groups are terrible for:

- Diagnosing slow sales
- Validating inventory decisions

- Setting pricing confidence
- Determining whether your booth is "failing"

Consume carefully.

Read with skepticism.
Observe patterns, not emotions.
Never outsource your judgment to a comment section.

A Reality Check Before We Go Further
If you've been using social media as your primary feedback loop, this chapter may feel uncomfortable.

That's intentional.

Because before you can fix a booth, you have to stop confusing noise for information.

The market is not speaking through social media.
It's speaking through your sales numbers, your turnover rate, your space productivity, and your customer behavior.

And that's where we're going next.

Chapter Takeaway
Social media groups feel like market truth because they amplify emotion, not accuracy. Consensus is comforting—but it is not evidence. Vendors who rely on group sentiment to guide decisions surrender control without realizing it.

Looking Ahead
In the next chapter, we'll shift away from memory and noise and into something far more reliable: measurable booth performance. Because once you stop listening to the crowd, you can finally hear what your booth is actually telling you.

What Your Booth Is Actually Telling You When You Start Listening

Most vendors don't believe they're ignoring their booth.

They believe they're paying attention.

> They watch people walk by.
> They notice when the register feels quiet.
> They feel the difference between a "good day" and a bad one.

The problem isn't that vendors aren't observing.
The problem is that they're listening to the wrong signals.

Feelings, impressions, and anecdotes are seductive because they're immediate. They give you something to react to. But they're also unreliable, inconsistent, and heavily influenced by mood, memory, and outside noise.

Your booth, on the other hand, is remarkably honest.

It reports on its performance every single month. Quietly. Consistently. Without drama.

Most vendors just haven't learned how to read the report.

Why Feelings Are the Worst Booth Metric

When sales slow down, vendors rarely say, "My performance indicators have shifted."

They say:

- "It feels dead."
- "Traffic feels off."
- "People are just browsing."

Those statements aren't lies—but they aren't measurements either.

- A booth can *feel* slow and still be profitable.

- A booth can *feel* busy and still be inefficient.
- A booth can *feel* disappointing simply because expectations haven't adjusted.

Feelings are reactive. They change day to day. They're influenced by weather, personal stress, online conversations, and memory. They also tend to exaggerate negative outcomes while minimizing stable ones.

If you've ever had a decent sales month that still felt discouraging, you already understand this.

Your booth doesn't run on feelings.
It runs on math.

Until you separate emotion from evaluation, every decision you make will feel heavier than it needs to be.

Sales Are Not the Same Thing as Performance

This is where many experienced vendors get tripped up.

Sales feel like the obvious metric. Money came in—or it didn't. End of story.

But sales alone don't tell you how well your booth is working. They only tell you that *something* happened.

Performance answers a different question:

How efficiently did your booth use the space, inventory, and capital available to it?

A booth can produce sales and still underperform.
A booth can feel "okay" and still be wasting opportunity.
A booth can survive for years while slowly bleeding momentum.

This is why two vendors with similar sales numbers can have very different outcomes. One feels constantly stressed. The other feels steady and in control.

The difference isn't luck.
It's efficiency.

Performance tells you whether your booth is doing the best it can with what you've given it—or whether it's coasting on habits that no longer serve it.

The Three Numbers That Matter More Than Anything Else

You don't need complex spreadsheets to understand your booth. You need clarity on a few core signals.

There are many metrics vendors *can* track. But only three truly matter at this stage.

1. Inventory Age

How long items sit before selling.

This number reveals more than almost anything else.

Old inventory:

- Ties up capital
- Occupies space
- Lowers booth energy
- Signals misalignment with current buyers

If a significant portion of your booth has been present for months—or years—your booth is telling you something very clearly.

And it's not saying "wait longer."

2. Sell-Through Rate

How much of what you bring in actually sells.

A booth that constantly restocks but never clears space is not growing. It's accumulating.

Sell-through tells you whether:

> New inventory is replacing old inventory
> Or piling on top of it

Low sell-through creates the illusion of productivity. You're busy. You're sourcing. You're restocking.

But the booth remains stuck.

Movement matters more than activity.

3. Revenue Per Space

How much each square foot or section earns.

Booths are not abstract. They are physical, finite resources.

If one area consistently underperforms while another carries the load, the booth is showing you where adjustments are needed.

Ignoring that imbalance doesn't make it fair. It just makes it expensive.

> These three numbers don't judge you.
> They inform you.

Once you understand them, decision-making becomes lighter— not heavier.

Inventory Age: The Quietest Warning Signal

Inventory age doesn't shout. It whispers.

It looks like:

- Items you stop noticing
- Pieces you dust but don't reconsider
- Displays you rearrange instead of replacing

Old inventory rarely feels urgent. That's why it's dangerous.

Each item that overstays its usefulness reduces the booth's ability to respond to change. It blocks new opportunities before they even arrive.

This isn't about "bad items."
It's about *misaligned* items.

An item can be:

- Well-made
- Well-priced
- Perfectly fine

And still be wrong for your booth *right now*.

Inventory age is not a moral failing. It's a signal.

The longer you ignore it, the louder it becomes.

Booth Space Is Not Neutral
Many vendors treat booth space as passive.

They think:
"If something sells, great. If not, it'll just sit."

But booth space is not neutral. It either works for you or against you.

Every square foot:

- Competes with every other item
- Influences how shoppers move
- Affects perception of value
- Determines what gets noticed

When underperforming inventory occupies prime space, it doesn't just fail on its own—it suppresses everything around it.

This is why booths with "good stuff" can still feel dead.

Space allocation is strategy, whether you intend it to be or not.

Why Rearranging Feels Productive (and Isn't)
When sales slow, vendors often respond with movement.

Shelves shift.
Displays rotate.
Items migrate.

Rearranging feels productive because it's visible effort. It gives the sense that something is being done.

But rearranging doesn't change:

- Inventory age

- Price resistance
- Category relevance
- Buyer demand

It changes appearance, not performance.

Rearranging is useful *after* decisions are made—not instead of them.

If nothing leaves the booth, nothing improves.

Activity Is Not the Same as Progress

This is one of the most uncomfortable realizations for experienced vendors.

Being busy does not mean moving forward.

You can:

> Source constantly
> Rearrange weekly
> Restock aggressively

And still be stuck.

Progress requires subtraction as much as addition.

Removing inventory:

- Frees capital
- Restores clarity
- Sharpens focus
- Forces decisions

If your booth never shrinks, it can't evolve.

The Cost of Waiting Shows Up in Space, Not Just Sales

Waiting doesn't look dramatic.

It looks like:

- Items overstaying
- Space stagnating

- Energy flattening

Over time, this erodes confidence—not because you're failing, but because you're not acting.

Action restores agency.

Once you stop waiting for the booth to "turn around" and start responding to what it's telling you, momentum returns surprisingly fast.

Not overnight. But measurably.

Avoiding the Panic Pivot

Reading your booth honestly does *not* mean reacting impulsively.

One slow month does not demand a full reset.
One quiet week does not mean failure.

Patterns matter more than moments.

Performance should be evaluated over time:

- Consistent stagnation
- Repeated non-movers
- Predictable underperformance

The goal is deliberate adjustment, not emotional reaction.

When vendors panic, they often overcorrect—and create new problems in the process.

Clarity prevents panic.

Responsibility Is Not Blame

This chapter may feel heavy for some readers. That's natural.

Taking responsibility doesn't mean you caused the market.
It means you're choosing to respond to it.

Blame is paralyzing.
Responsibility is empowering.

Once you stop outsourcing outcomes to memory, groups, or circumstances, you regain control.

And control changes everything.

When the Booth Stops Feeling Hostile

Many vendors describe the market as hostile, unpredictable, or unfair.

That feeling often disappears once clarity replaces confusion.

When you know:

- What's working
- What isn't
- Why
- And what to change next

The booth stops feeling like a judgment.

It becomes a tool.

Chapter Takeaway

Your booth is always communicating. Not through feelings, comments, or crowd sentiment—but through performance. When you replace emotion with observation and nostalgia with data, the market stops feeling mysterious and starts feeling manageable.

Looking Ahead

Now that you can *see* what your booth is telling you, the next question becomes unavoidable:

What do you change first?

In the next chapter, we'll address inventory focus, density, and the order of decisions—so you don't fix the wrong problem first.

Fix the Right Problem First: Inventory Focus, Density, and Decision Order

Clarity is dangerous without order.

That might sound backwards, but it's one of the most common reasons experienced vendors stay stuck even after they finally understand what's wrong. Once you can clearly see stagnation, misalignment, and inefficiency, the urge to *fix everything immediately* becomes almost irresistible.

> You notice slow movers.
> You notice crowded shelves.
> You notice categories that feel tired.

And suddenly every part of the booth feels like the problem.

That's when vendors make their most expensive mistakes—not because they're wrong, but because they fix the *wrong thing first*.

This chapter exists to slow that moment down.

Because not all booth problems carry the same weight. And when you address them out of order, you don't create momentum—you create churn.

The Most Common Mistake After Gaining Clarity

After reading the last chapter, some vendors will feel something click into place. They'll recognize inventory age. They'll see inefficiencies. They'll understand that the booth has been communicating clearly all along.

And then they'll walk into their booth and start rearranging.

> Or repricing.
> Or adding new categories.
> Or buying more inventory to "freshen things up."

None of those actions are inherently wrong. But taken too early—or taken together—they dilute progress instead of creating it.

Clarity creates urgency.
Urgency creates movement.
Movement without order creates noise.

The goal isn't to do *something*.
The goal is to do the *right thing first*.

Why Inventory Is Always the First Lever

Everything in a booth traces back to inventory.

> Layout exists to display it.
> Pricing exists to move it.
> Signage exists to frame it.

If the inventory itself is misaligned, nothing built on top of it can compensate for that misalignment.

Vendors often want to skip this step because it's uncomfortable. Inventory represents time, money, effort, and identity. Removing or narrowing it can feel like admitting failure—even when it's simply responding to data.

But inventory is not a moral statement.
It is a tool.

And when the tool no longer fits the job, continuing to use it doesn't make you loyal—it makes you inefficient.

Until inventory is addressed, every other change remains fragile. A better layout will still showcase the wrong items. Better pricing will still struggle against weak demand. Better styling will still highlight pieces buyers aren't choosing.

Inventory is the root system of the booth. If it's tangled, everything above ground suffers.

Focus Before Expansion

When sales slow, vendors often expand instead of refine.

They add a new category.
They chase a trend.
They broaden their selection "just in case."

This feels proactive. It feels adaptive. And sometimes—briefly—it even creates a sales bump.

But expansion without focus rarely lasts.

A booth that sells a little of everything often sells *very little of anything*. Buyers don't experience it as variety—they experience it as confusion.

Focused booths do something powerful:

They tell buyers exactly who they're for.

That clarity reduces friction. Buyers move faster. Decisions feel easier. Confidence increases. And confidence sells.

Focus doesn't mean repetition or boredom. It means coherence. It means each piece reinforces the others instead of competing for attention.

A booth with fewer categories—but stronger identity—almost always outperforms a scattered booth with more inventory.

Focus isn't limitation.
It's leverage.

Understanding Inventory Density

Density is one of the least understood—and most mismanaged—elements of booth performance.

Inventory density isn't just "how full the booth is." It's how intentionally space is used relative to the inventory it holds.

Too much density overwhelms buyers.
Too little density makes the booth feel hollow or unfinished.

Both reduce sales.

Overfilled booths exhaust the eye. Buyers can't distinguish importance, so everything becomes noise. They skim instead of engage. They miss good items because there's no visual hierarchy guiding them.

Underfilled booths, on the other hand, feel tentative. They signal uncertainty. Buyers assume selection is limited or incomplete—even when quality is high.

Effective density creates rhythm.

It gives items room to breathe without losing momentum. It creates natural pauses, focal points, and movement paths that feel intuitive rather than forced.

Density isn't about maximizing how much you can physically fit. It's about maximizing how well buyers can *process* what they're seeing.

The Hidden Cost of Dead Space and Overcrowding
Dead space and overcrowding are often treated as aesthetic issues.

They're not.

They are performance issues.

And worse, they are *quiet* performance issues—ones that rarely announce themselves clearly, but steadily drain a booth's potential over time.

Dead space doesn't always look empty. Sometimes it looks neat. Sometimes it looks intentional. Sometimes it even looks "clean." But unless that space is actively supporting movement, visibility, or emphasis, it isn't neutral—it's idle.

Idle space breaks momentum.

Buyers do not move through booths randomly. They move in patterns, following visual cues, light, contrast, and perceived value. When they encounter areas that don't offer engagement or purpose, their pace increases. They skim instead of browse.

They disengage instead of explore. And once engagement is lost, it is rarely regained within the same booth.

That moment matters more than most vendors realize. Once a buyer mentally checks out, they don't slow back down for the next shelf. They carry that disengagement forward, often through the rest of the booth.

Overcrowding creates the opposite—but equally damaging—effect.

Instead of disengagement, it creates fatigue.

When every surface is full, no surface stands out. When every item competes for attention, buyers stop trying to evaluate altogether. The brain shifts from *considering* to *escaping*. Even strong pieces—items that would sell well on their own—get overlooked because they're buried inside visual noise.

This is why vendors so often say, "I have great stuff, but nobody seems to notice it."

They're usually right.

> The problem isn't quality.
> It's compression.

Buyers don't struggle because items aren't good enough. They struggle because nothing has been given permission to matter more than anything else.

Dead space and overcrowding are symptoms of the same root issue: inventory decisions that haven't been made yet.

When inventory hasn't been narrowed or removed, space is forced to compensate. One area becomes overloaded because everything has to live somewhere. Another becomes underutilized because nothing clearly *belongs* there anymore. The booth loses its internal logic.

This is also why rearranging rarely solves the problem. Rearranging redistributes pressure—it doesn't relieve it.

Neither dead space nor overcrowding resolves itself through movement alone.
Only intentional subtraction and reallocation fix this.

Every square foot in a booth should be able to answer a simple question:

What does this space help sell?

> Not what sits there.
> Not what used to be there.
> Not what *might* sell someday.

What does it actively support right now?

If the answer is unclear—or if the space exists simply because something needed a place to sit—it isn't working. And space that isn't working doesn't stay neutral. It quietly undermines everything around it.

Good density creates a sense of purpose. It gives buyers visual cues about what matters, what's featured, and where to pause. It creates contrast so important items feel intentional instead of accidental. It allows the booth to guide attention rather than compete for it.

When density is right, buyers don't feel rushed or overwhelmed. They feel oriented.

And orientation is what turns interest into movement, and movement into sales.

Why Rearranging Feels Productive (and Isn't)

Rearranging is seductive because it looks like action.

> Shelves move.
> Displays shift.
> The booth looks different.

And sometimes different feels better—briefly.

But rearranging without inventory decisions only changes the scenery. It doesn't change the outcome.

Rearranging becomes a form of avoidance when it replaces removal, narrowing, or reallocation. It keeps everything in play, just shuffled.

That's why vendors can rearrange the same booth dozens of times without meaningful improvement.

Rearranging is useful *after* decisions are made. It helps reinforce focus, support density, and guide buyer movement.

Before that, it's just motion.

The Correct Order of Booth Decisions

This is the core of the chapter—and the framework vendors should return to whenever their booth feels stuck.

There is an order that creates clarity and momentum. Skipping steps doesn't save time. It creates confusion.

1. Remove What Isn't Working

This includes aged inventory, repeat non-movers, and categories that no longer align with buyer behavior. Removal frees space, capital, and mental bandwidth.

2. Refine Inventory Focus

Decide what the booth is actually about now—not what it used to be or what you wish it were. Narrow categories. Strengthen identity.

3. Adjust Density

Once focus is clear, density can be calibrated. Space becomes intentional instead of accidental.

4. Reallocate Space

Give performing categories room to expand. Shrink or eliminate underperformers.

5. Only Then: Pricing, Signage, and Styling

These elements work best when they reinforce good decisions—not when they're used to compensate for bad ones.

This order reduces overwhelm. It turns vague dissatisfaction into manageable steps.

Most importantly, it prevents wasted effort.

Why Subtraction Creates Momentum

Vendors often fear removal because it feels like loss.

But subtraction is what restores movement.

Removing inventory forces clarity. It sharpens decisions. It makes space visible again—not just physically, but mentally.

A booth that never shrinks cannot evolve. It just accumulates history.

Progress requires letting go of what no longer serves the current version of the booth. That isn't failure—it's adaptation.

Momentum doesn't come from adding more weight. It comes from removing resistance.

Making Changes Without Triggering Panic

One of the hardest skills for experienced vendors to develop is restraint.

Not in effort—but in reaction.

When clarity arrives, it often brings an emotional surge with it.

- Frustration over missed signals.
- Regret over money already spent.
- Urgency to *fix this now*.

That emotional spike is understandable. It's human. But it becomes dangerous when it's allowed to dictate decisions.

Panic doesn't usually look like chaos.

It looks like overcorrection.

A vendor panics and cuts too deeply, stripping the booth of categories that still had potential.

Or panics and buys too aggressively, flooding the space with new inventory before the old problems are resolved.
Or panics and abandons a direction entirely without giving buyers time to respond to changes.

In each case, the result isn't clarity.

It's instability.

Instability is expensive because it disrupts patterns—both yours and the buyer's. A booth that changes too often never feels settled. Buyers sense that lack of confidence, even if they can't articulate it. The booth feels experimental instead of intentional.

Deliberate change works differently.

Deliberate change is measured. It's paced. It respects patterns rather than moments.

> One slow month does not define a category.
> One fast sale does not validate a direction.

Performance lives in consistency, not spikes.

This is why time-bound decisions are so powerful. They introduce structure into change, which is exactly what panic removes.

Instead of asking, *"Should I get rid of this category?"* ask: ***"What happens if I remove this category for 60 days?"***

Instead of asking, *"Should I rework my whole booth?"* ask: ***"What changes if I reduce density in this one section for the next two months?"***

These questions don't demand immediate judgment. They invite observation.

Time-bound experiments do three critical things.

First, they reduce emotional risk.
Decisions don't feel permanent, so you're less likely to protect them out of pride or fear. You can act honestly instead of defensively.

Second, they create clean data.
When changes are isolated and intentional, results become easier to read. You're no longer guessing which adjustment caused which outcome.

Third, they preserve confidence.
You remain in control of the process instead of feeling pulled along by results. Adjustments feel strategic rather than reactive.

Panic thrives on uncertainty.
Structure eliminates it.

When vendors move too fast, they often lose trust in their own judgment. Every result feels suspect. Every dip feels catastrophic. Good decisions get abandoned prematurely. Momentum becomes fragile because it's never allowed to stabilize.

Slow, intentional changes rebuild that trust.

You begin to recognize what works because you gave it time to work. You stop second-guessing every outcome. Decisions feel calmer—not because the booth is perfect, but because you understand it.

You're no longer reacting to the booth.

You're managing it.

What Momentum Actually Feels Like
Momentum is often misunderstood.

Many vendors expect it to feel exciting—busy, fast, affirming. They expect energy, urgency, and constant movement. But real momentum feels quieter than that.

> It feels stable.
> It feels predictable.
> It feels like decisions require less emotional labor.

Momentum shows up first in how the booth *feels* to manage.

Inventory begins to move with less resistance. You no longer wonder *if* something will sell—only *when*. Restocks feel intentional instead of urgent. You bring items in because they fit the booth's direction, not because you're trying to fill space, chase a slow week, or manufacture activity.

The booth stops arguing with you.

Instead of second-guessing every choice, you begin to recognize patterns. You trust what works because it keeps working. You trust what doesn't because it consistently doesn't. That trust removes friction from decision-making. You're no longer negotiating with yourself every time you consider a change.

This shift fundamentally alters the emotional experience of selling.

The market stops feeling hostile.

Not because conditions suddenly improve, but because confusion disappears. When you understand what's working, what isn't, and why, uncertainty loses its power. Slow periods stop feeling ominous. Strong periods stop feeling fragile. Both become part of a larger, understandable rhythm.

You're no longer asking, *"Is my booth failing?"*
You're asking, *"What adjustment makes sense next?"*

That distinction matters.

Momentum also changes how you respond to setbacks. A quiet week no longer triggers panic. A slow category doesn't feel like a personal indictment. You already know where the levers are, and you know you don't have to pull all of them at once.

This is why real momentum feels calm.

It isn't driven by constant activity. It isn't measured by how busy you feel. It's measured by how rarely you feel rushed, reactive, or unsure.

That's real momentum.

Not speed.
Not volume.
Not nonstop movement.

Momentum is clarity that sustains itself.

And once it's established, it's surprisingly difficult to lose—as long as you continue honoring the order of decisions that created it. When you respect that order, progress compounds quietly, steadily, and with far less stress than most vendors believe is possible.

Chapter Takeaway
You don't need to work harder.
You don't need to add more.

You need to fix problems in the right order.

Inventory focus and density create leverage. When those foundations are solid, everything else becomes easier—and far more effective.

Looking Ahead
Now that you know what to remove, narrow, and rebalance, the next question becomes unavoidable:

How much inventory should your booth actually carry—and how do you avoid overloading it again?

In the next chapter, we'll address inventory math, capital efficiency, and sustainable restock strategy—so growth doesn't quietly turn back into clutter.

Inventory Math: Capital, Capacity, and Sustainable Restock

Most vendors don't think of inventory as math.

They think of it as instinct.

They buy what they like. They restock what feels empty. They react to slow weeks by "bringing in something new." They react to good weeks by doubling down. None of this feels irrational while it's happening. In fact, it often feels responsible—like staying engaged, staying flexible, staying proactive.

But over time, something strange happens.

> The booth stays full.
> The effort stays high.
> The stress never really goes away.

And money feels tighter than it should.

This is where instinct reaches its limit.

Not because instinct is wrong—but because instinct isn't designed to manage **systems**. It's designed to respond to moments. Inventory, however, is not a moment-to-moment decision. It's a living system made up of capital, space, time, and buyer behavior. When any one of those elements is misunderstood, the entire system starts working against you.

This chapter exists to replace instinct with structure—not to turn you into a spreadsheet manager, but to give your intuition something solid to stand on.

Because once inventory math is understood, a surprising thing happens:

> Restocking stops feeling urgent.
> Buying stops feeling emotional.
> And growth stops turning back into clutter.

The Myth of "More Inventory = More Sales"

One of the hardest beliefs for experienced vendors to release is the idea that more inventory naturally leads to more sales.

It feels logical. More choices should mean more opportunities. More surface area should mean more engagement. More volume should increase the odds that something catches a buyer's eye.

And in the early stages of a booth, this is often true.

When a booth is underfilled or newly launched, adding inventory almost always improves performance. Buyers notice the expansion. Selection improves. The booth feels alive. Sales respond.

That early success is what plants the myth.

The problem is that this relationship does not scale indefinitely.

At a certain point—usually without warning—adding more inventory stops increasing sales and starts **diluting** them. Items compete instead of complement. Attention fragments. Buyers slow down, then disengage. Turnover drops even as volume rises.

This is where vendors get confused.

From their perspective, they're doing everything right:

- The booth is full.
- The quality is strong.
- They're actively sourcing.
- They're showing up and adjusting.

So when sales stall, the instinctive response is to add more—new categories, new styles, new price points—anything to re-ignite movement.

But inventory does not create demand.

It only responds to it.

Demand exists independently of how much you stock. Buyers don't buy because you have more items. They buy because something resonates, feels easy to choose, and fits a moment they're already in.

When inventory exceeds that demand, performance doesn't collapse dramatically. It erodes quietly. That's what makes this myth so dangerous. There's no single failure point—just a slow tightening of margins, cash flow, and confidence.

Understanding this is the first step toward sustainable inventory control.

Capacity vs. Saturation

Every booth has a capacity.

Not a physical limit—an operational one.

Capacity is the amount of inventory your booth can carry *effectively* while still doing three things at the same time:

- Maintaining visual clarity
- Supporting buyer decision-making
- Turning capital at a healthy pace

As long as those three conditions are met, adding inventory can still help. It can increase engagement, improve selection, and give buyers more opportunities to connect with what you sell.

Saturation begins the moment one of those conditions quietly breaks.

And that's what makes saturation so dangerous.

It doesn't announce itself with chaos. It doesn't always look messy. In fact, many saturated booths look impressive. They're full, styled, cohesive, and stocked with quality pieces. From the outside—sometimes even to the vendor—it appears that everything is working.

But internally, the system has already started to strain.

Saturation is not about *too much stuff*.
It's about *too much pressure in the same decision space*.

When inventory crosses the booth's true capacity, buyers don't consciously register it as overload. Instead, their behavior changes in subtle, predictable ways. Decision thresholds rise. Browsing replaces choosing. Interest lingers without converting.

This is why saturation is often mistaken for "a slow market."

> The booth didn't fail.
> It didn't lose relevance.
> It didn't suddenly attract the wrong buyers.

It overfilled.

Why Saturation Often Follows Success

One of the most counterintuitive truths of booth selling is that saturation frequently appears *after* a good run.

> Sales are strong.
> Restocking feels justified.
> Space is available.
> Confidence is high.

So inventory grows.

At first, nothing breaks. In fact, things may even improve. More product means more movement—until it doesn't. The moment demand stops increasing at the same rate as inventory, pressure builds.

But instead of recognizing that the booth has reached capacity, most vendors interpret the slowdown incorrectly.

They assume:

- Buyers are being more cautious
- The market has softened
- They need to refresh inventory again

So they add more.

This is how good booths quietly become saturated ones.

Saturation doesn't come from neglect.
It comes from momentum that isn't constrained.

The Compression Effect

Saturation works by compression, not clutter.

When too many items exist within the same visual and cognitive range, buyers stop evaluating pieces individually. The brain shifts from *consideration* to *scanning*. Instead of asking, "Do I want this?" buyers unconsciously ask, "Is it worth deciding right now?"

Often, the answer becomes no.

This is where vendors notice changes that are difficult to explain:

- Customers spend more time in the booth but buy less
- Items are handled frequently but rarely purchased
- Sales happen only when price becomes the deciding factor

Nothing feels broken.
Everything feels heavier.

That weight is compression.

And compression always favors delay over decision.

Clear Signs You've Crossed Into Saturation

Saturation doesn't show up as a single event. It reveals itself through patterns.

If several of these feel familiar, capacity has likely been exceeded:

- Sales flatten or decline even as inventory increases
- Buyers browse deeply but leave empty-handed
- Strong items sell slowly unless discounted
- Removing inventory feels risky instead of relieving
- Restocking feels heavier, not exciting

- Cash feels tight despite consistent traffic

These signs are often misread as effort problems.

They're not.

They're structure problems.

Why Saturation Feels Safer Than Space

One reason vendors resist acknowledging saturation is emotional.

Full booths feel secure.

Inventory represents work, time, identity, and investment. Empty space feels like exposure. It triggers fear—fear of missed sales, fear of looking understocked, fear of not being taken seriously.

Saturation feels productive by comparison.

But this is an illusion.

A saturated booth protects feelings at the expense of function. It replaces clarity with comfort. And comfort is expensive when it interferes with decision-making.

Space is not absence.
Space is permission.

- Permission for items to stand out.
- Permission for buyers to pause.
- Permission for decisions to happen.

Capacity is not about filling space.
It's about protecting that permission.

Capacity Is Not Fixed—but It Must Be Earned

Capacity *can* grow.

But it grows only when demand grows first.

Traffic increases.
Sell-through improves.
Categories prove consistency.

Only then can inventory expand without compression.

When inventory grows ahead of demand, saturation is inevitable—no matter how strong the product mix is.

This is why capacity must be respected, not tested.

Testing capacity by overfilling doesn't increase it. It obscures the signal that tells you where the limit actually is.

The Question That Matters

Instead of asking:
"How much inventory can I fit?"

The better question is:
"How much inventory can my booth support without resisting buyers?"

When buyers move easily, decide confidently, and return consistently, capacity is being respected.

When decisions slow, hesitation rises, and inventory piles up, saturation has already arrived.

Recognizing that moment—and responding by subtracting instead of adding—is one of the most important skills an experienced vendor can develop.

Because once capacity is honored, inventory stops fighting you.

And when inventory stops fighting you, everything else in the booth gets easier.

Why Money Gets Trapped in Inventory

Most vendors don't think of themselves as cash-poor.

They think of themselves as inventory-rich.

The booth is full. The shelves are stocked. There's value everywhere you look. From a distance, it appears that the business is healthy—even successful. After all, money didn't disappear. It just turned into things.

And yet, when it's time to restock intentionally, handle an unexpected expense, or pivot in response to buyer behavior, money suddenly feels unavailable.

That tension is the first sign that inventory has stopped working as a tool and started behaving like a holding cell.

Because inventory is not money.

It is **potential money**—and potential only becomes real when time cooperates.

Inventory Is Borrowed Capital

Every dollar sitting in inventory is borrowed from your future self.

It's money you've already spent, waiting to be returned through a buyer's decision. Until that happens, it can't be used anywhere else. It can't adapt. It can't respond. It can't protect you.

This is why two vendors with similar booth sizes and comparable sales numbers can experience completely different levels of financial stress.

One has inventory that cycles.
The other has inventory that waits.

The difference isn't intelligence, effort, or sourcing skill.

It's velocity.

Inventory that moves returns capital. Inventory that waits traps it. And trapped capital quietly narrows your options month after month.

Time Is the Most Expensive Inventory Cost

Most vendors think about inventory cost only at the moment of purchase.

What did I pay?
What do I need to sell it for?
What's my margin?

But time is a cost too—and it compounds.

The longer inventory sits:

- The less flexible that money becomes
- The more emotionally attached you grow to it
- The harder it becomes to make clear decisions about it

An item that sits for six months isn't just unsold. It has accumulated weight.

That weight shows up as hesitation:

- "I can't move that yet—I need to get my money back."
- "It might sell in the right season."
- "Someone will want this eventually."

Sometimes those statements are true.

But time doesn't care.

Every month an item remains unsold, it increases the *true* cost of holding it—not in dollars, but in lost opportunity. That same money could have cycled multiple times through faster-moving inventory. It could have reduced stress. It could have created momentum instead of friction.

This is why vendors often feel busy but stagnant.

Their capital isn't gone.
It's immobilized.

Why Trapped Money Changes Behavior

When money gets trapped in inventory, it doesn't just affect finances—it reshapes decision-making.

Vendors compensate in predictable ways:

They buy cheaper items to stretch limited cash.
They hesitate to remove slow movers because "too much is tied up already."
They add new categories to hedge against stagnation.

Each response feels logical in isolation.

Together, they reinforce the trap.

Cheaper inventory often turns slower.
Hesitation preserves underperformers.
Category expansion increases saturation.

The booth becomes heavier—not because inventory is bad, but because capital is no longer circulating.

This is the moment where vendors often say:

"I'm selling, but I don't feel like I'm getting ahead."

That feeling is accurate.

The booth is working.
The system is not.

The Emotional Attachment Problem

One of the least discussed costs of trapped inventory is emotional.

The longer an item sits, the more it becomes part of the booth's identity—and by extension, part of the vendor's identity. Time invested becomes justification. Effort becomes defense. Removal begins to feel like admitting a mistake.

But inventory does not know how hard you worked to acquire it.

It only knows whether buyers choose it.

This is where experienced vendors struggle more than beginners. Beginners let go easily because they haven't invested as much yet. Experienced vendors have history tied up in their stock.

That history clouds judgment.

Inventory doesn't need to be bad to be wrong *right now*.
And being wrong right now is not the same as being wrong forever.

But trapped capital makes patience feel risky—and risk makes people cling tighter, not loosen their grip.

Why Waiting to "Get Your Money Back" Rarely Works

One of the most damaging beliefs vendors carry is the idea that holding inventory longer increases the chance of recovery.

In reality, the opposite is often true.

As time passes:

- Buyer attention shifts
- Trends evolve
- Comparables change
- Your booth context moves on

An item that didn't resonate when it was fresh rarely gains strength by aging quietly in place. More often, it requires *greater* concession later—through discounting, bundling, or removal—than it would have earlier.

Waiting doesn't preserve value.
It postpones recognition.

And postponement is expensive.

The Real Cost of Being Inventory-Rich

Being inventory-rich feels stable.
Being cash-flexible *is* stable.

Cash flexibility allows you to:

- Restock confidently instead of emotionally
- Respond to sell-through signals quickly
- Say no to inventory that doesn't fit
- Adjust without panic

When capital is trapped, every decision feels heavier because the margin for error shrinks. The booth becomes something you must protect instead of something that supports you.

This is why inventory math matters.

Not to optimize profits.
Not to maximize margins.

But to keep your capital moving.

Because money that moves gives you options.
Money that waits quietly takes them away.

Bridge Forward

Once you understand that inventory is capital on a timer, the next question becomes unavoidable:

How fast should that capital come back?

That's where **inventory velocity and sell-through** take over—not as metrics to obsess over, but as signals that tell you whether your booth is breathing or holding its breath.

Inventory Value vs. Inventory Velocity

Most vendors know the value of their inventory.

> They know how much they've spent.
> They know what pieces are "worth."
> They often know—roughly—what they could get back *eventually*.

What most vendors don't know is how fast that value actually returns.

Inventory value answers a static question:

"How much money is sitting in my booth?"

Inventory velocity answers a dynamic one:

"How often does that money come back to me?"

And velocity is what keeps a booth alive.

A booth can be full of valuable inventory and still be unhealthy. Value without movement creates stagnation. It looks impressive on paper and exhausting in practice. Capital stays locked while decisions get heavier and risk tolerance shrinks.

Velocity, on the other hand, creates momentum even at lower price points. When inventory moves predictably, capital cycles. Confidence grows. The booth feels responsive instead of rigid.

This is why two vendors with similar inventory values can experience radically different outcomes.

One feels stuck.
The other feels steady.

The difference isn't taste, effort, or sourcing skill.

It's how quickly inventory turns back into usable capital.

Why Volume Is a Poor Substitute for Movement
When sales slow, many vendors respond by increasing volume.

> They add more pieces.
> They broaden categories.
> They "give buyers more to choose from."

This feels proactive. It also feels safer than removing inventory.

But volume without velocity does not increase opportunity—it dilutes it.

Adding inventory does not speed up buyer decisions. In many cases, it slows them down. When too many options exist, buyers delay choice instead of making one. They browse longer, touch more, and commit less.

This is the moment where vendors often say:

"People love my booth—they just aren't buying."

That statement is usually true.

But love without conversion is not the goal.

Velocity exposes this problem quickly. When items move slowly despite high engagement, the issue isn't interest. It's friction.

And friction always favors delay.

Why Vendors Defend High-Value, Low-Velocity Inventory

One of the hardest inventory decisions involves items that are *good* but slow.

These pieces often:

- Took time to source or restore
- Carry higher price points
- Represent taste, skill, or identity

They feel important.

So vendors give them time. They justify their presence. They wait for the "right buyer."

Sometimes that buyer exists.

But velocity doesn't ask whether an item is good.

It asks whether it's working.

An item that sells once a year may technically be profitable—but it still traps capital for eleven months. If that same capital could have cycled multiple times through faster inventory, the booth would be stronger overall.

This is where experienced vendors struggle most.

They aren't wrong about quality.
They're just overvaluing patience.

Velocity Is Contextual, Not Absolute

Velocity does not mean everything must sell fast.

Different categories tolerate different timelines. Seasonal items wait. Specialty pieces linger. Higher price points breathe slower.

The mistake vendors make is comparing across categories instead of within them.

Velocity should always be evaluated relative to:

- Category norms

- Price point expectations

- Booth role (anchor pieces vs. fillers)

The goal is not speed.
The goal is **predictability**.

When you can reasonably anticipate how long something should take to sell, inventory decisions become calmer and more accurate.

Unpredictability—not slowness—is what creates stress.

Sell-Through: The Metric That Replaces Guesswork
Sell-through is how velocity becomes visible.

It doesn't require spreadsheets or perfect tracking. It doesn't demand precision. It simply answers a practical question:

"How much of what I bring in actually sells within a reasonable amount of time?"

When sell-through is healthy:

- Restocking feels obvious
- Capital cycles smoothly
- Buying decisions feel grounded

When sell-through weakens:

- Inventory accumulates
- Restocking becomes emotional
- Doubt replaces clarity

Sell-through removes guesswork because it forces honesty.

It doesn't care how much you like an item.
It doesn't care how good a deal it was.
It doesn't care how long you've had it.

It only reflects buyer behavior.

What 'Reasonable Time' Actually Means

"Reasonable time" is where most vendors get stuck.

They either expect everything to sell too quickly—or allow things to linger indefinitely.

Reasonable time depends on context:

- Fast-moving categories may need weeks
- Mid-range items may need months
- Seasonal items need full cycles

The key is not choosing a deadline.

The key is choosing a *window*.

If items consistently exceed their expected window, sell-through is weak—even if occasional sales happen.

A single sale does not validate a category.
A pattern does.

This is why sell-through should be reviewed in ranges, not moments.

Why Sell-Through Tells You When *Not* to Restock

One of sell-through's greatest strengths is restraint.

It doesn't just tell you what to buy more of.
It tells you when to stop.

If inventory in a category hasn't moved proportionally, adding more only increases saturation. Restocking becomes rescue instead of maintenance.

This is where many vendors sabotage themselves.

>They restock based on hope instead of evidence.
>They respond to slow periods by adding pressure.
>They mistake activity for progress.

Sell-through removes that temptation.

It gives you permission to wait.
To observe.
To let space exist without panic.

Sell-Through Is Not a Judgment

A slow category is not a failure.
A fast category is not a guarantee.

Sell-through is information—not identity.

It tells you where capital flows easily and where it resists. It shows you what buyers understand and what they hesitate to choose. It reveals whether your booth is aligned with current demand or clinging to past success.

Most importantly, it restores trust in decision-making.

When sell-through is understood, you stop arguing with yourself.

>You don't guess.
>You don't chase.
>You don't overcorrect.

You respond.

Why Velocity Creates Calm

When inventory velocity is healthy, everything else softens.

>Buying becomes intentional.
>Restocking becomes boring.
>Cash feels available.
>Space feels purposeful.

You stop asking:

>*"What should I try next?"*

And start asking:

>*"What supports what's already working?"*

That shift is where momentum stabilizes.

Not because the booth is perfect.
But because it's readable.

Transition Forward

Once velocity and sell-through are clear, restocking stops being reactive.

It becomes maintenance.

That's where we're headed next.

Inventory-to-Rent Ratios (Without Dogma)

At some point, every vendor encounters a rule.

>Three times rent.
>Four times rent.
>Six times rent.

These rules circulate because they're simple—and because they work *just often enough* to feel authoritative.

The problem is that inventory-to-rent ratios aren't prescriptions.

They're **diagnostics**.

A booth carrying three times rent in inventory can be healthy or struggling. A booth carrying six times rent can be thriving or suffocating. The ratio alone doesn't tell the story—it just points to where questions should be asked.

What matters is:

>How fast that inventory turns
>How focused the categories are

How much capital you can comfortably leave tied up

Rigid formulas fail experienced vendors because experience introduces variability. Category mix matters. Price point matters. Market matters. Personal risk tolerance matters.

Instead of asking, *"Am I at the right multiple?"* the better question is:

"Is my current inventory level supporting or restricting my ability to operate calmly?"

If inventory creates pressure—financial or emotional—it's too heavy, regardless of the number.

Restocking as Maintenance, Not Rescue

Healthy restocking feels boring.

That sentence makes some vendors uncomfortable, but it shouldn't. Boredom is not stagnation. Boredom is what stability feels like when systems are working.

When restocking is healthy, it doesn't spike adrenaline. It doesn't feel urgent. It doesn't arrive with pressure or relief. It happens quietly, predictably, and without drama.

That's not a lack of engagement.
That's control.

Rescue restocking, on the other hand, feels *important*.

> It feels necessary.
> It feels urgent.
> It feels like doing something to fix a problem.

And that's why it's so dangerous.

The Two Restock Cycles

Most vendors operate in one of two restock cycles, even if they don't realize it.

Rescue Restocking is reactive.
Maintenance Restocking is responsive.

They may look similar from the outside, but internally they produce completely different outcomes.

Rescue Restocking

Rescue restocking usually begins with discomfort.

Sales slow.
Energy drops.
Doubt creeps in.

The booth doesn't feel broken, but it feels *off*. Instead of pausing to evaluate sell-through or capacity, the vendor responds emotionally.

They restock because:

- The booth feels empty in spots
- Something "new" might spark interest
- Activity feels better than waiting

This restock often includes:

- New categories "to try"
- Larger quantities than usual
- Inventory chosen for novelty, not fit

For a moment, it feels like progress.

> The booth looks fresh.
> There's movement.
> There's hope.

But the underlying issue hasn't been addressed.

Sell-through hasn't improved.
Capacity hasn't expanded.
Demand hasn't changed.

So the new inventory enters an already strained system.

That's when saturation tightens.

Rescue restocking doesn't solve slow sales.
It amplifies the conditions that caused them.

Maintenance Restocking

Maintenance restocking feels almost dull by comparison.

It happens because something sold.
Not because something feels wrong.

It follows patterns instead of reacting to feelings. It replaces inventory intentionally rather than adding pressure. Quantities are modest. Categories stay focused. Density remains consistent.

Maintenance restocking asks:

- What sold consistently?
- What moved within its expected window?
- What fits the booth's current direction?

And just as importantly:

- What didn't sell enough to justify replacement?

Maintenance restocking respects restraint.

It accepts that not every empty space needs to be filled immediately. It allows the booth to breathe without interpreting space as failure.

This is where confidence quietly rebuilds.

Why Rescue Restocking Feels So Tempting

Rescue restocking feels productive because it creates visible change.

Boxes arrive.
Shelves get rearranged.
The booth looks different.

That visual activity tricks the brain into believing progress is being made—even when the system underneath hasn't changed.

Maintenance restocking doesn't offer that same emotional payoff. There's no dramatic transformation. No "fresh start" feeling. Just steady replacement.

This is why vendors who are used to operating under pressure often struggle with stability.

Stability doesn't reward effort emotionally.
It rewards discipline.

The Cost of Emotional Restocking

Every emotional restock increases three risks:

1. **Capital Risk**
   Money gets committed without confirmation that it will return on schedule.
2. **Density Risk**
   Inventory accumulates faster than space or demand can absorb it.
3. **Decision Fatigue**
   Each restock adds complexity, making future decisions harder instead of easier.

Over time, emotional restocking trains vendors to distrust their own judgment. When results are inconsistent, confidence erodes. Every restock feels like a gamble instead of a choice.

That's when vendors start saying:

"I don't know what works anymore."

The booth becomes noisy—not just visually, but mentally.

Why Boring Is the Goal

When restocking becomes boring, several things are happening at once:

- Sell-through is predictable
- Capacity is respected
- Capital is cycling
- Decisions require less emotional labor

You're no longer guessing whether something *might* work. You're responding to what already has.

This is the moment when vendors often worry they're becoming complacent.

They aren't.

They're becoming operational.

Growth that lasts is not exciting from the inside. It's measured. It's repeatable. It's quiet.

Letting Space Exist Without Panic

One of the most difficult skills for experienced vendors is allowing space to exist temporarily.

Empty space triggers fear:

- Fear of missed sales
- Fear of looking understocked
- Fear of appearing inactive

But space is not failure.

Space is information.

> It tells you what sold.
> It tells you where pressure released.
> It gives buyers room to see what remains.

Maintenance restocking allows space to exist until it earns its replacement. Rescue restocking smothers that signal.

When space is immediately filled without reflection, you lose data.

The Question That Changes Everything

Instead of asking:
"What should I bring in next?"

Maintenance restocking asks:
"What has already earned its replacement?"

That question alone eliminates most bad buying decisions.

> It removes urgency.
> It removes panic.
> It restores trust.

Bridge Forward

Once restocking becomes maintenance instead of rescue, the next danger isn't panic.

It's drift.

Because even stable booths can slowly overload themselves if nothing prevents expansion from creeping back in.

That's why the next step isn't buying better.

It's installing guardrails.

How Overloading Sneaks Back In

Overloading rarely feels like a decision.

It feels like a series of small, reasonable exceptions.

> One extra piece because it was a great deal.
> One new category because it *might* work.
> One additional shelf because the space could handle it.

None of these moments feel reckless. In isolation, each one makes sense. They don't trigger alarm because they don't look like overfilling—they look like optimism.

That's what makes regression so quiet.

Vendors don't return to clutter because they forget what works. They return because success lowers their guard. Confidence replaces caution. Momentum removes friction. And without constraints, expansion creeps back in under the guise of growth.

This is why many vendors experience a familiar cycle:

Clarity → momentum → expansion → saturation → confusion.

Not because the strategy was wrong—but because it was never protected.

Why Success Is More Dangerous Than Struggle

Struggle forces discipline.

When money is tight and space is limited, vendors make careful decisions. Inventory is evaluated. Categories are questioned. Space is defended.

Success removes that pressure.

> Sales are steady.
> Capital feels available.
> Space opens up.
> **Standards loosen.**

The booth absorbs more inventory not because it needs it—but because it can. This is when vendors begin buying ahead of demand instead of responding to it. The booth slowly fills with *potential* instead of performance.

Nothing collapses.
Nothing breaks.

But capacity is crossed again.

The "Just One More" Trap

Overloading almost always happens through accumulation, not overhaul.

No single item causes saturation.
No single restock creates clutter.

It's the cumulative effect of "just one more."

> Just one more piece in a strong category.
> Just one more category to experiment with.
> Just one more restock before reviewing sell-through.

Each addition slightly increases pressure. Over time, those small pressures compress decision space until buyers begin resisting again.

This is why vendors often don't recognize saturation until it's fully re-established.

By the time discomfort returns, inventory decisions are already buried under volume.

Why Rearranging Feels Like a Fix (Again)

When overloading sneaks back in, vendors often respond the same way they did before clarity arrived: rearranging.

> Shelves move.
> Displays shift.
> Flow changes.

Rearranging feels corrective because it creates visible change. But once again, it redistributes pressure instead of relieving it. The booth looks different, but the system underneath remains overloaded.

This is how vendors end up cycling through layouts instead of decisions.

Without constraints, rearranging becomes a substitute for subtraction.

Setting Inventory Guardrails

Guardrails exist to prevent regression—not to limit growth.

They are not rules meant to punish creativity. They are systems designed to protect momentum when confidence returns and caution fades.

Guardrails remove emotion from decisions by answering questions *before* they arise.

When guardrails exist, you don't ask:
"Should I bring this in?"

You ask:
"Does this fit within the structure I already trust?"

That shift is everything.

What Guardrails Actually Do

Effective guardrails do three things simultaneously:

1. **They slow accumulation**
   Inventory can only grow when something justifies its place.
2. **They preserve clarity**
   Categories stay legible. Density stays intentional.
3. **They reduce decision fatigue**
   You stop negotiating with yourself on every purchase.

Guardrails don't eliminate judgment.
They support it.

Examples of Practical Guardrails

Guardrails don't need to be complex. They need to be *enforced*.

Common forms include:

- **Category caps**
  A fixed number of categories allowed in the booth at one time.
- **Dollar caps per category**
  Inventory value ceilings that prevent overinvestment.
- **One-in / one-out systems**
  New inventory enters only when something leaves.
- **Time-based reviews**

Inventory must earn its continued presence at scheduled intervals.

The specific guardrail matters less than consistency. A simple system followed reliably will outperform a perfect system followed occasionally.

Soft Guardrails vs. Hard Guardrails

Not all guardrails need to be rigid.

Soft guardrails guide behavior:

- "I won't add a new category without removing one."
- "I won't restock unless sell-through supports it."

Hard guardrails enforce limits:

- Fixed shelf counts
- Dollar ceilings
- Physical space restrictions

Most vendors benefit from a mix of both.

Soft guardrails preserve flexibility.
Hard guardrails prevent drift.

Why Guardrails Protect Confidence

One of the least obvious benefits of guardrails is emotional.

When guardrails exist, decisions feel lighter. You're no longer responsible for *every* choice. The system carries some of that weight.

That protection matters most during good periods—when temptation is high and consequences feel distant.

Guardrails prevent success from undoing itself.

The Real Goal: A Booth That Self-Corrects

The ultimate purpose of inventory guardrails is not control.

It's self-correction.

A well-guarded booth doesn't need dramatic overhauls. Small deviations are caught early. Pressure is relieved before saturation returns. Momentum stabilizes instead of spiking and collapsing.

This is what sustainable success actually looks like.

Quiet.
Predictable.
Manageable.

Closing the Loop
When inventory math is understood...
When capacity is respected...
When velocity guides decisions...
When restocking is maintenance...
And when guardrails prevent drift...

The booth stops fighting you.

Inventory becomes cooperative instead of demanding. Capital becomes flexible instead of trapped. Decisions become calm instead of urgent.

That's not luck.
That's structure.

What Sustainable Inventory Actually Feels Like
Sustainable inventory doesn't feel exciting.

It feels calm.

> You know what to buy.
> You know what to pass on.
> You know when to wait.

> Money flows.
> Space breathes.
> Decisions settle.

That calm is not complacency.
It's control.

Chapter Takeaway

Inventory math isn't about precision.

It's about protection.

> Protecting capital.
> Protecting clarity.
> Protecting momentum.

When inventory is aligned with capacity and demand, growth stops collapsing back into clutter—and selling stops feeling like a fight.

Looking Ahead

Once inventory is controlled, the next lever becomes unavoidable:

Pricing.

> Not discounts.
> Not markdowns.

But how buyers *perceive* value—and why friction quietly kills otherwise good booths.

That's where we're headed next.

Price Isn't the Problem (Friction Is)

By the time vendors reach this chapter, most of them are already confident they know how pricing works.

> They've priced for years.
> They've tested numbers.
> They've run sales.
> They've adjusted margins.
> They've listened to advice.

And yet—pricing still feels like the most fragile part of the booth.

Sales slow, and price becomes the suspect.
Momentum dips, and tags get questioned.
Confidence wavers, and numbers start moving.

What makes pricing so frustrating is that it *almost* works. Nothing looks obviously wrong. Prices aren't outrageous. Inventory isn't junk. Buyers are still browsing. Compliments still happen.

But decisions stall.

This chapter exists to explain why.

> Not by introducing new formulas.
> Not by offering discount strategies.
> Not by telling you to race to the bottom or climb to the top.

But by reframing pricing as buyers actually experience it.

Because pricing doesn't fail when it's "too high."
It fails when it creates hesitation.

Buyers don't resist spending money nearly as much as they resist uncertainty. They hesitate when they don't feel confident enough to decide—and price is often blamed simply because it's the most visible variable.

In reality, price is rarely the problem.

Friction is.

Friction in how items are grouped.
Friction in how value is communicated.
Friction in how choices are presented.
Friction in how safe a decision feels in the moment.

When friction exists, even fair prices stall.
When friction is removed, prices stop being questioned.

This chapter is not about convincing buyers.
It's about making decisions easier.

Once that happens, pricing stops feeling fragile—and starts working quietly in the background, where it belongs.

The Lie Vendors Are Told About Pricing

Most vendors are taught a simple equation early on:

Lower prices sell faster.

It sounds practical. It feels logical. And in certain narrow situations—clearance tables, distressed inventory, urgent cash needs—it can even be true.

But as a guiding principle, it quietly causes more damage than almost any other belief in booth selling.

Because price is rarely the reason a buyer hesitates.

Uncertainty is.

Vendors experience this disconnect constantly. They hear comments like:

"I love this."
"This is really cool."
"I'll think about it."

And their mind immediately jumps to price. Too high. Too ambitious. Too optimistic for this market.

So they adjust.

They shave margins.
They undercut themselves.
They discount before anything is actually wrong.

And still—buyers hesitate.

That's because buyers don't evaluate price the way vendors do.

Vendors see price as math.
Buyers experience price as risk.

A buyer standing in an antique mall is not comparing your $42 item to the $38 version they might find elsewhere. They are deciding whether this purchase feels *safe*. Safe emotionally. Safe financially. Safe psychologically.

They're asking questions silently, often without realizing it:

Is this priced fairly?
Is this worth deciding right now?
Will I regret this later?
Can I explain this purchase to myself—or someone else?

If those questions are not answered effortlessly, the buyer pauses. And when buyers pause in antique environments, they usually don't come back.

This is why pricing issues are so often misdiagnosed.

From the vendor's perspective:

"People like my booth but aren't buying."

From the buyer's perspective:

"I'm not confident enough to decide."

Lowering price does not automatically create confidence. In many cases, it does the opposite. When prices drop without clarity, buyers don't feel relieved—they feel suspicious.

Why is this cheaper?
What am I missing?
Should I wait?

This is the part vendors struggle with emotionally.

They believe they are removing barriers.
Buyers feel like something shifted without explanation.

That gap is where friction lives.

The lie vendors are told is that pricing is a lever you pull to force movement.

It's not.

Price is a signal. And when that signal conflicts with presentation, context, or consistency, buyers don't interpret it as opportunity—they interpret it as uncertainty.

This is why two booths selling similar items at similar prices can experience completely different outcomes.

One booth converts effortlessly.
The other attracts interest but no commitment.

The difference is not the number on the tag.

It's whether the price feels *supported*.

Supported by:

- Clear category identity
- Consistent logic
- Visual hierarchy
- Trust built through presentation

When those elements are present, buyers don't debate price—they accept it.

When they're absent, no price feels safe enough.

This is also why experienced vendors often struggle more with pricing than beginners.

Beginners price conservatively. They assume they're wrong. They defer to the market. Ironically, this sometimes creates clearer signals because everything aligns at the lower end.

Experienced vendors, however, accumulate range.

Different sourcing methods.
Different eras.
Different costs.
Different emotional investments.

Without realizing it, pricing logic fragments. The booth still looks good. Inventory is strong. But price stops telling a coherent story.

Buyers feel that fragmentation instantly—even if they can't articulate it.

And when buyers can't read a booth, they hesitate.

That hesitation gets blamed on price.

So vendors adjust the number instead of addressing the friction underneath it.

This chapter exists to dismantle that reflex.

Because pricing problems are rarely solved by lowering prices.

They're solved by making decisions easier.

And ease—not cheapness—is what actually sells.

How Buyers Actually Decide in Booth Environments

Most vendors imagine buyer decision-making as deliberate.

A customer enters the booth.
They browse.
They evaluate.
They compare.
They decide.

That model assumes time, clarity, and emotional neutrality.

None of those conditions exist in an antique mall.

Booth environments create a very different kind of decision process—one that is fast, fragile, and easily disrupted. Buyers are not operating with focused intent. They are operating under cognitive load.

By the time a buyer reaches your booth, they've already made dozens—sometimes hundreds—of micro-decisions.

> Do I turn down this aisle?
> Do I stop here?
> Do I pick this up?
> Do I read this tag?
> Do I keep moving?

Each decision consumes mental energy. And mental energy is finite.

This matters because buying is not a logical endpoint—it's an emotional one. When cognitive resources run low, the brain defaults to the safest option available.

In antique environments, the safest option is almost always delay.

> "I'll come back."
> "I'll think about it."
> "I need to look around more."

These aren't objections. They're exit strategies.

Buyers don't leave because they dislike something. They leave because deciding feels expensive.

This is why vendors often misread buyer behavior.

> A customer spends time in the booth.
> They touch items.
> They smile.
> They comment positively.

From the outside, everything looks right.

But internally, the buyer is negotiating risk:

> Is this the best option?
> Is this fairly priced?
> Am I missing something better nearby?
> Do I need to commit right now?

If those questions are not answered quickly, the brain conserves energy by postponing the decision.

That postponement feels rational to the buyer.
It feels personal to the vendor.

This is where frustration builds.

Vendors assume buyers are price-sensitive.
Buyers are actually *energy-sensitive*.

Every additional step required to understand an item increases the likelihood of hesitation:

> Unclear pricing logic
> Too many similar choices
> Dense displays
> Inconsistent presentation
> Tags that explain nothing or too much

Each of these forces the buyer to think.

And thinking slows buying.

This is amplified by the nature of antique malls themselves.

Unlike traditional retail, there is no unified pricing structure. No shared brand. No assumed standard. Buyers know this, which means they approach every booth with a low baseline of trust.

> They expect inconsistency.
> They expect surprises.
> They expect to have to work a little.

What they don't want is to work *too much*.

When effort crosses an invisible threshold, the buyer disengages—not consciously, but behaviorally. They move on to preserve mental bandwidth.

This is why buyers often remember booths emotionally but not specifically.

> "That place had cool stuff."
> "There was a booth I liked."

But they can't remember what they didn't decide on.

Because no decision was actually made.

The most important thing to understand is this:

Buyers are not asking, "Is this worth the price?"
They are asking, "Is this worth deciding right now?"

Those are very different questions.

Price only becomes central when everything else is clear. When clarity exists—about category, value, and logic—buyers accept price as part of the story.

When clarity is missing, price becomes the scapegoat.

This is also why booths with strong aesthetics but weak structure struggle.

> They attract attention.
> They invite browsing.
> They create interest.

But interest without clarity creates exhaustion.

The buyer's brain says:
"I like this—but I don't want to sort this out right now."

So they don't.

They leave with the intention of returning, which almost never materializes. Not because they forgot—but because the decision still feels unresolved.

Understanding this shifts how pricing problems should be approached.

> The goal is not to convince buyers.
> The goal is to reduce the cost of deciding.

When decision cost drops, price resistance softens automatically.

When decision cost remains high, no discount feels good enough.

This is the environment your pricing operates in—not a calm comparison shop, but a mentally crowded, emotionally noisy space where ease wins every time.

And that's why the next section matters more than any pricing formula.

Because friction—not price—is what actually stops the sale.

Pricing Friction: The Invisible Sales Killer

Pricing friction is not a single mistake.

It's the accumulation of small signals that tell a buyer, *"This will take effort."*

The problem is that none of these signals feel dramatic. They don't look like errors. Most of them are completely reasonable choices when viewed individually. But together, they create resistance that buyers respond to instinctively.

And instinct always chooses delay.

Pricing friction exists whenever a buyer has to *interpret* instead of *recognize*.

The moment a buyer stops seeing and starts thinking, momentum breaks.

This is why pricing friction is so often invisible to vendors. Vendors already know their logic. They understand their sourcing. They remember their costs. Buyers don't have that context. They encounter price as a surface signal—and when that signal is unclear, the brain hesitates.

Here are the most common sources of pricing friction inside otherwise good booths.

Too Many Similar Prices Without Hierarchy

When buyers see multiple items clustered in the same price range without a clear reason for the difference, decision cost spikes.

$38
$42
$45
$48

None of those numbers are unreasonable. But without visible hierarchy—size, quality, rarity, function—the buyer must mentally rank them.

Which one is better?
Why is this one more?
Is the difference meaningful?

That effort feels small—but it compounds. The brain responds by postponing the decision entirely.

Buyers don't choose *between* similar prices.
They choose *out*.

Clear pricing works best when it forms steps, not noise. Buyers should feel progression intuitively. When everything lives in the same narrow band, nothing feels anchored.

Inconsistent Pricing Logic Across Categories

One of the most damaging friction sources is inconsistency.

A booth might have:

- Handmade items priced confidently
- Vintage items priced conservatively
- Decor priced emotionally
- Furniture priced defensively

Each decision makes sense in isolation.

Together, they create confusion.

Buyers don't need to understand your sourcing—but they do need to sense coherence. When similar items feel priced under different rules, trust erodes. Not consciously, but enough to trigger hesitation.

The buyer starts asking:
"Why is *this* priced like that?"

And once that question appears, the booth has already lost momentum.

Price Clustering Without Anchors

When everything in a booth feels "mid-range," buyers struggle to orient themselves.

> There's no obvious entry point.
> No clear stretch piece.
> No anchor that frames the rest.

Anchors don't exist to sell.
They exist to contextualize.

A higher-priced piece makes mid-range items feel safer.
A lower-priced piece gives buyers permission to start.

Without anchors, buyers feel like they're stepping into a conversation already in progress—without knowing where to enter.

So they don't.

Tags That Explain Nothing (or Everything)

A price tag that only lists a number forces interpretation.

> What is this?
> Why is it priced this way?
> Is this special?

On the other extreme, overly detailed tags overwhelm.

Buyers don't want education.
They want reassurance.

The best tags answer one quiet question:
"Why is this reasonable?"

Not defensively. Not aggressively. Just enough to let the buyer relax.

When tags fail to do that, buyers pause.

Displays That Don't Justify Cost

Pricing friction increases dramatically when presentation and price feel mismatched.

> A $60 item displayed casually feels expensive.
> A $60 item displayed intentionally feels expected.

This is where many vendors unknowingly sabotage themselves.

They price appropriately—but display generically.

The buyer doesn't think, "This is overpriced."
They think, "I don't know why this costs that."

And uncertainty always wins.

Why Rearranging Doesn't Fix Friction

When sales slow, vendors often rearrange displays to "freshen" the booth.

But rearranging without reducing friction simply redistributes it.

> The same questions remain.
> The same inconsistencies persist.
> The same decision costs exist.

The booth looks different—but it doesn't read easier.

This is why vendors experience brief upticks followed by the same stall. Visual novelty masks friction temporarily. It doesn't remove it.

The Moment Friction Takes Over

The defining moment of pricing friction is not rejection.

It's hesitation.

> The buyer likes the item.
> They respect the booth.
> They can afford the price.

They just don't feel confident enough to *decide*.

So they don't.

And because antique environments are saturated with alternatives, hesitation almost always ends the transaction.

The buyer doesn't need to say no.

They just need to keep walking.

The Core Truth

Pricing friction is not about numbers.

It's about clarity.

When pricing is clear, buyers don't negotiate internally.
They accept or decline.

When pricing is unclear, buyers delay.
And delay is death in booth selling.

Removing friction doesn't require lowering prices.

It requires making prices *readable*.

When buyers can understand pricing at a glance—without effort—resistance drops naturally.

That's when price stops being the problem.

And that's what allows the next section to land:

Why discounts don't solve friction—and often make it worse.

Why Discounts Don't Fix Bad Pricing

Discounts are seductive because they feel decisive.

> They create movement.
> They signal action.
> They offer the illusion of control.

When sales slow, a discount feels like doing something concrete. It produces visible change without requiring uncomfortable decisions about inventory, layout, or structure.

That's why vendors reach for it so quickly.

The problem is that discounts don't remove friction.

They only mask it.

A discount works when a buyer already trusts the booth and simply needs a final nudge. In that context, the price reduction feels like permission. The decision was nearly made—the discount just accelerates it.

But when friction exists, discounts change the *question* instead of answering it.

Instead of:
"Is this worth deciding?"

The buyer asks:
"Why is this discounted?"

That question is dangerous.

Because now the buyer is not evaluating value—they're evaluating risk.

> Is something wrong?
> Is this old?
> Is it overpriced normally?
> Should I wait for a bigger markdown?

In booths where pricing logic is already unclear, discounts increase uncertainty instead of reducing it. Buyers don't feel relief. They feel caution.

This is why many vendors experience the same pattern:

> A discount produces a brief spike.
> Then sales slow again.
> Then a deeper discount feels necessary.

Not because discounts don't work—but because they were applied to the wrong problem.

Discounts don't fix confusion.
They amplify it.

When buyers can't easily understand why something costs what it does, lowering the price doesn't create clarity. It introduces suspicion.

And suspicion delays decisions.

How Discounts Train Hesitation

Frequent discounts teach buyers a silent lesson:

Don't decide yet.

Even when buyers like something, they hesitate—because waiting has been rewarded before. The booth becomes a place to monitor instead of a place to commit.

This is especially damaging in antique mall environments, where buyers already expect variability. When discounts appear without structure, buyers stop trusting price signals altogether.

> They don't know what's real.
> They don't know what's temporary.
> They don't know when a price means "fair" versus "flexible."

So they wait.

Why "Sale Booths" Feel Unsafe

Booths that rely heavily on discounts often feel chaotic, even when inventory quality is high.

Prices shift.
Tags change.
Signs multiply.

Buyers sense instability.

Instead of thinking, "I'm getting a deal," they think, "I need to be careful."

That caution overrides excitement.

A buyer who feels cautious doesn't browse freely.

They don't explore.
They don't commit.
They scan.
They protect.
They leave.

This is why discounts feel powerful but underperform long-term.

They attract attention.
They don't build trust.

When Discounts Actually Work
Discounts are effective when:

Pricing logic is already clear
Value is already established
The booth feels stable and intentional

In those conditions, a discount doesn't create doubt—it resolves hesitation.

But when discounts are used as a primary tool instead of a strategic one, they erode confidence on both sides.

The vendor starts questioning pricing.
The buyer starts questioning value.

Nobody wins.

The Real Cost of Discount Dependency

Over time, reliance on discounts creates three problems:

Margins shrink
Buyers delay decisions
Vendors lose pricing confidence

The booth becomes reactive instead of readable. Decisions are driven by fear instead of structure.

And worst of all, discounts become a crutch that prevents vendors from addressing the actual issue: friction.

The Better Alternative

The solution to slow sales is not a lower number.

It's a clearer signal.

When buyers understand what they're seeing—why it exists, how it's grouped, and how it's priced—price resistance fades naturally.

Discounts should never be the first response.
They should be the final polish on a system that already works.

Otherwise, they don't fix the problem.

They hide it.

Perceived Value vs. Stated Price

Buyers do not experience price in isolation.

They experience it in context.

The number on a tag is not evaluated on its own—it's interpreted through everything surrounding it: presentation, placement, grouping, and the emotional tone of the booth itself.

This is why two identical items can sell at different prices in different booths.

The difference isn't the number.
It's the story the environment tells.

Perceived value is not about convincing buyers something is "worth it." It's about removing the tension between desire and justification. Buyers want to feel aligned with their choice—not defensive about it.

> When perceived value is high, price feels reasonable—even generous.
> When perceived value is low, price feels aggressive—even when it's fair.

This is the gap vendors often miss.

They price based on cost, margin, or comparables.
Buyers price based on confidence.

Context Creates Permission

Buyers need permission to buy.

Not literal permission—but emotional permission.

They want to feel that choosing this item makes sense within the environment they're standing in. That permission comes from context.

Context answers questions without forcing thought:

> What category is this?
> How special is it?
> What role does it play?
> Why does it belong here?

When context is clear, price becomes secondary. When context is weak, price carries the entire burden—and collapses under it.

This is why random placement kills perceived value.

A strong item placed without intention feels overpriced.
The same item placed with purpose feels obvious.

Grouping Changes Everything

Items don't compete individually.

They compete in groups.

When items are grouped intentionally, buyers stop evaluating them in isolation and start evaluating the category as a whole. This reduces friction.

> A single item at $55 feels expensive.
> A group of similar items priced from $38–$75 creates a spectrum.

Suddenly, $55 feels middle-of-the-road instead of risky.

> This is not manipulation.
> It's clarity.

Buyers need reference points. Without them, every price feels like a question mark.

Scarcity Is Not Rarity

Vendors often confuse scarcity with rarity.

> Rarity is about supply.
> Scarcity is about signal.

A rare item can feel common if it's buried.
A common item can feel scarce if it's framed correctly.

Scarcity is created by focus.

When too many items compete for attention, nothing feels special. When fewer items are presented with intention, buyers feel urgency—not because they're pressured, but because the environment suggests decisiveness.

That decisiveness makes price easier to accept.

Presentation Must Match Price

Buyers instinctively compare price to presentation.

> A higher price demands structure.
> A lower price tolerates looseness.

When these are mismatched, friction appears.

> A premium item displayed casually triggers doubt.
> A modest item displayed thoughtfully feels elevated.

This is why pricing problems are often display problems in disguise.

Vendors lower prices to compensate for presentation gaps—when strengthening presentation would have solved the issue more cleanly.

Why Explanation Beats Justification

Perceived value is strongest when buyers feel informed—not persuaded.

Explanation is quiet.
Justification is defensive.

A simple line like:
"Hand-thrown stoneware, local artist"

Does more work than:
"Priced fairly for the quality"

The first gives context.
The second raises suspicion.

Buyers don't want to be sold to.
They want to feel smart about their choice.

The Silent Equation

Buyers don't calculate value consciously, but they follow a consistent internal equation:

Does this make sense here?
Does it fit the environment?
Does it feel intentional?

If the answer is yes, price becomes acceptable.
If the answer is no, price becomes the excuse.

This is why perceived value must be built before pricing is questioned.

Price is not the start of the conversation.

It's the conclusion.

When Raising Prices Improves Sell-Through

Raising prices feels backward.

When sales slow, the instinct is to remove resistance. To be safer. More competitive. More reasonable. Raising prices feels like adding friction instead of reducing it.

And yet—experienced vendors see it happen all the time.

Prices go up.
Sales improve.

Not because buyers suddenly want to spend more—but because the signal becomes clearer.

Price is not just a cost.
It's information.

And when prices are too low for the context they're presented in, they send the wrong message.

Low Prices Can Increase Risk

Buyers are not suspicious by default—but they are sensitive to inconsistency.

When an item feels underpriced relative to its environment, buyers don't celebrate. They hesitate.

> Why is this so cheap?
> What's wrong with it?
> Is this authentic?
> Is this comparable to what I've seen elsewhere?

These questions introduce doubt.

And doubt slows decisions.

In antique environments, low prices can trigger more internal debate than moderate ones. Buyers expect variability—but they still rely on pricing to help them orient themselves.

When prices don't match perceived value, the buyer's trust in the booth weakens.

Raising Prices as Clarification

Raising prices works when it aligns price with context.

> The item didn't change.
> The booth didn't change.
> The presentation didn't change.

But the signal did.

A higher price can:

- Affirm quality
- Confirm intention
- Reduce internal negotiation

Instead of thinking, "Is this too much?" the buyer thinks, "This is what this costs."

That shift matters.

Buyers don't want to argue with price. They want to accept it or reject it cleanly. Ambiguous pricing forces them to negotiate internally—and negotiation is exhausting.

Why This Works Better for Experienced Vendors

Experienced vendors often undervalue themselves.

They have better sourcing.
Stronger curation.
More refined taste.

But because they remember cost—and effort—they hesitate to price confidently. They fear being "that booth." They fear overreaching.

So they soften.

They price to avoid rejection.

Ironically, this creates more hesitation than confidence would have.

Raising prices when presentation and context already support them removes that hesitation. The booth feels decisive. Buyers respond to decisiveness.

The Price Floor Problem

Many booths suffer from an unintentional price floor.

Everything clusters around what feels safe.
Nothing stretches.
Nothing anchors.

When prices rise slightly, that floor lifts—and suddenly the booth reads more clearly. Lower-priced items feel accessible. Mid-range items feel justified. Higher items feel intentional instead of risky.

Price structure emerges.

And structure sells.

When Raising Prices Fails

Raising prices does not fix confusion.

If pricing logic is inconsistent...
If presentation is weak...
If categories are muddled...

Higher prices amplify friction instead of resolving it.

Raising prices works only when clarity already exists. It is not a correction tool—it's a signal amplifier.

The Real Reason It Feels Uncomfortable

Raising prices feels uncomfortable because it removes hiding places.

> You can't blame the market.
> You can't blame bargain hunters.
> You can't blame competition.

You have to trust your structure.

That trust is difficult—but powerful.

When prices align with perceived value, sell-through improves not because buyers are paying more—but because they are deciding faster.

And speed—not generosity—is what drives momentum.

When Price Stops Being the Question

When pricing is clear, something unexpected happens.

Buyers stop talking about price.

> They don't ask if it's fair.
> They don't hesitate at the tag.
> They don't need convincing.

They decide—or they don't—quickly and cleanly.

That decisiveness is the real goal.

> Not higher prices.
> Not lower prices.
> Not constant discounts.

Decisions.

When friction is removed, price becomes a conclusion instead of an obstacle. Buyers accept it as part of the environment, just like lighting or layout. It no longer demands attention.

This is when vendors notice a shift:

> Sales feel steadier.
> Restocking feels safer.
> Confidence returns.

Not because the booth is perfect—but because it's readable.

> Price clarity restores trust.
> Trust reduces hesitation.
> Hesitation is what actually kills sales.

Once price stops being the question, the booth stops fighting itself.

Chapter Takeaway

Pricing isn't about numbers.

It's about signals.

When pricing aligns with presentation, structure, and buyer psychology, resistance fades. Not all at once—but consistently.

> The booth becomes easier to navigate.
> Decisions become lighter.
> Momentum stabilizes.

Price doesn't sell.
Clarity does.

Looking Ahead

Once pricing friction is removed, the final barrier to consistent sell-through isn't inventory or price.

It's **trust**.

Trust in the booth.
Trust in the brand.
Trust that what buyers see today will still make sense tomorrow.

That's where we're going next.

Trust Is the Multiplier
Inconsistency Is the Tax

By this point in the book, most vendors have already done something difficult.

> They've stopped blaming the market.
> They've let go of nostalgia.
> They've learned to ignore noise.
> They've listened to what their booth is actually telling them.
> They've fixed problems in the right order.
> They've brought inventory under control.
> They've removed pricing friction.

On paper, the booth should be working.

And yet—for many vendors—it still feels fragile.

Sales happen, but they don't feel dependable. Good weeks don't create confidence; they create relief. Slow weeks don't feel contextual; they feel threatening. Every dip raises the same quiet question:

"Is this actually stable?"

That tension is not a failure of effort or execution.

It's a trust problem.

> Not trust in yourself.
> Not trust in your inventory.
> Not trust in the market.

Trust in the booth as a system.

Buyers don't just evaluate items. They evaluate environments. They don't just ask whether something is worth the price—they ask whether deciding *here* feels safe. When that safety exists, decisions happen faster, resistance softens, and momentum stabilizes. When it doesn't, hesitation returns—even when everything looks right.

This is why two booths with similar inventory, similar pricing, and similar foot traffic can produce wildly different results. One converts steadily. The other stalls. The difference isn't quality or hustle.

It's trust.

Trust is the invisible multiplier that determines whether all the work you've done so far compounds—or constantly has to be re-earned.

And inconsistency is the invisible tax that quietly eats away at it.

This chapter is not about branding, personality, or creating emotional attachment. It's about predictability, coherence, and reliability—how buyers read them, how vendors accidentally break them, and why trust builds more slowly than friction but pays off far longer.

If Chapter 7 was about making decisions easier, this chapter is about making decisions feel safe.

Because once friction is removed, trust becomes the deciding force.

And nothing else in booth selling works without it.

Buyers Are Not Evaluating Items (They're Evaluating Risk)
By the time a buyer reaches your booth, they are not asking whether your inventory is good.

They are asking whether deciding here feels safe.

This distinction matters more than most vendors realize—because buyers don't consciously experience risk as fear. They experience it as hesitation. A pause. A feeling of "not yet." And in antique mall environments, hesitation is almost always terminal.

Buyers don't walk into a booth intending to analyze it. They walk in carrying mental fatigue. They've already made dozens of small decisions—where to turn, where to stop, what to glance at, what to ignore. Each one costs energy. Each one quietly raises the bar for the next decision.

By the time they're holding an item, the decision isn't "Do I like this?"
It's "Do I trust this choice enough to commit right now?"

That trust is not emotional warmth. It's structural confidence.

Buyers are evaluating risk across multiple layers at once:

- Will this price still make sense later?
- Does this booth feel consistent, or unpredictable?
- If I pass this up, will I regret it—or feel relieved?
- Does buying here feel intentional, or impulsive?

None of these questions feel dramatic. They don't register as doubt. They simply increase the cost of deciding. And when decision cost rises, the brain defaults to delay.

This is why so many vendors experience the same frustrating pattern:

> Shoppers linger.
> They browse carefully.
> They comment positively.

And then they leave.

Nothing went wrong. No objection was raised. No rejection occurred. The buyer simply did not feel enough certainty to spend their limited decision energy here.

That outcome is often misdiagnosed as price resistance, inventory issues, or market softness. But more often, it's a trust gap.

Trust, in this context, is not about credibility or reputation. It's about predictability. Buyers trust environments that behave consistently—where signals align, expectations are met, and decisions feel supported rather than exposed.

When buyers trust a booth, they don't feel like they're gambling. They feel like they're choosing.

And choice feels safe.

This is why two booths selling similar inventory at similar prices can perform wildly differently. One converts steadily. The other stalls. The difference isn't taste, sourcing, or effort. It's whether the booth reduces perceived risk—or quietly amplifies it.

Risk doesn't have to be real to be influential. Buyers don't need evidence that something is wrong. They only need uncertainty about whether something is right.

In antique environments, that uncertainty compounds quickly. There is no brand umbrella. No standardized pricing logic. No assumed consistency. Buyers know this. They approach every booth with a cautious baseline, scanning for signals that say, "You can trust this space."

When those signals are clear, decisions happen faster—even at higher prices.

When those signals are mixed, buyers don't negotiate internally. They disengage.

This is why trust becomes the multiplier once friction is removed.

Pricing clarity helps buyers understand the cost.
Trust helps them accept it.

Friction makes decisions harder.
Lack of trust makes decisions feel risky.

Risk—not price—is what buyers are actually avoiding.

This chapter is not about how to make buyers like your booth more.

It's about how to make choosing inside it feel safe.

Because once buyers trust the environment, everything else works better:

> Prices feel steadier.
> Inventory moves more predictably.
> Momentum stabilizes instead of spiking and collapsing.

Trust doesn't create excitement.
It creates permission.

And permission is what turns browsing into buying.

What Booth Trust Actually Is (And Isn't)

When vendors hear the word *trust*, many of them picture personality.

Friendliness. Warmth. Storytelling. Vibe.

They assume trust is something you build by being likable, approachable, or memorable. And while those things can enhance a buying experience, they are not what creates trust inside a booth.

Trust is not emotional connection.

Trust is **predictability**.

Buyers trust environments that behave the way they expect them to behave. Where signals are consistent. Where decisions don't feel like traps. Where nothing unexpected happens after the moment of commitment.

That's why trust is structural, not personal.

A buyer can trust a booth without ever speaking to the vendor. A buyer can distrust a booth run by the nicest person in the building.

Because buyers aren't evaluating character. They're evaluating systems.

They are asking, often subconsciously:

- Does this booth make sense as a whole?

- Do prices behave consistently?

- Do similar items follow similar rules?

- Does the presentation match what's being asked?

- Does this feel stable—or experimental?

When those questions are answered quietly and consistently, trust forms without effort. When they're not, hesitation creeps in—even if nothing is technically "wrong."

This is where many vendors get confused.

They think trust is about *liking* the booth.
But buyers like many booths.

Trust is about whether the booth feels **reliable enough to decide in.**

> A booth can be charming and still feel risky.
> A booth can be understated and feel solid.

The difference is coherence.

What Trust Is Not

Trust is not novelty.
Newness can attract attention, but it does not create safety. In fact, constant novelty often reduces trust because it signals instability. Buyers don't know what's normal—or what will still make sense later.

Trust is not excitement.
Excitement speeds browsing, not buying. It encourages exploration, not commitment. Buyers slow down and decide only when excitement gives way to confidence.

Trust is not volume.
More inventory does not feel more trustworthy. It often feels less so. When too many items compete for attention, buyers lose their ability to orient themselves—and orientation is a prerequisite for trust.

Trust is not explanation.
Overexplaining prices, sourcing, or value often signals insecurity. Buyers don't need justification. They need clarity.

What Trust Actually Looks Like

Trust shows up as ease.

Buyers don't stop to decode the booth. They don't search for patterns. They don't question whether they're missing something. They simply move through the space with confidence.

They understand:

> What this booth sells
> What matters here
> What's special
> What's expected

Nothing surprises them in a bad way.

Prices feel aligned with presentation. Categories feel intentional. Groupings feel logical. The booth feels like it knows what it's doing—and that certainty transfers to the buyer.

This is why trust is cumulative.

No single element creates it. But small inconsistencies erode it quickly.

A booth can survive one odd price.
One awkward display.
One experimental category.

But when those inconsistencies stack, buyers feel it immediately—even if they can't explain why.

And once trust wavers, buyers don't argue with the booth.

They leave.

Why Trust Feels Boring to Vendors

One of the reasons vendors undervalue trust is that it doesn't feel exciting from the inside.

A trustworthy booth feels:

> Steady.
> Predictable.
> Almost quiet.

That calm can feel like stagnation to a vendor who equates progress with change. But to buyers, that calm is safety.

Buyers don't reward booths for surprising them every visit. They reward booths for making sense every visit.

Trust is not built through constant reinvention.
It's built through consistency that earns belief over time.

And once belief exists, buyers stop re-evaluating every decision.

They don't wonder if the booth is "worth it."
They assume it is—and move on to choosing what they want.

That's when momentum stabilizes.

Not because the booth is flashy.
But because it's reliable.

Inconsistency: The Silent Sales Killer
Inconsistency rarely announces itself.

It doesn't look like a mistake. It doesn't feel reckless. Most of the time, it looks like reasonable flexibility—small adjustments made in good faith, based on experience, instinct, or effort.

That's what makes it so dangerous.

Inconsistency doesn't repel buyers.
It confuses them.

And confusion doesn't trigger rejection.
It triggers hesitation.

By the time a buyer hesitates, the sale is already lost.

The reason inconsistency is so effective at killing sales is that it attacks trust quietly. Each inconsistency adds a small amount of decision cost. On its own, that cost feels insignificant. But buyers don't experience inconsistencies individually—they experience them cumulatively.

They don't think, "This booth is inconsistent."
They think, "I don't feel settled here."

That feeling is enough to stop a decision.

The Five Most Common Forms of Booth Inconsistency

Most booths don't suffer from chaos. They suffer from *layered inconsistency*—multiple small mismatches that slowly erode confidence.

1. Pricing Inconsistency

Pricing inconsistency isn't about being "too high" or "too low."

It's about rules changing without explanation.

> Similar items priced under different logic
> Comparable pieces behaving differently
> Prices that feel emotional instead of structured

Buyers don't need to know your sourcing costs—but they need to sense that prices follow a pattern. When they can't find one, they assume risk.

And when buyers assume risk, they delay.

2. Category Inconsistency

Category inconsistency happens when a booth doesn't clearly declare what it's *about*.

Vintage mixed with modern without intention
Handmade beside mass-produced without framing
High-end pieces sitting next to casual fillers

Each of these choices can work—*if* they're supported. But when categories collide without explanation, buyers don't know how to evaluate anything.

They can't tell what standard to apply.

So they don't apply one at all.

They browse instead of deciding.

3. Quality Inconsistency

Quality inconsistency is subtle—and especially common among experienced vendors.

Strong pieces coexist with "just okay" ones.
Excellent items are diluted by filler.
Standouts lose power because they're not protected.

Buyers notice this instantly.

They don't articulate it as quality variation. They interpret it as uncertainty.

"If some of this is great, why is some of it here at all?"

That question raises risk—not because the booth is bad, but because it feels unresolved.

4. Presentation Inconsistency

Presentation inconsistency is one of the fastest ways to tax trust.

> A polished display next to a cluttered one
> Careful lighting beside dead zones
> Styled vignettes interrupted by dump spaces

Buyers read presentation as intent.

When intent fluctuates within the same booth, buyers struggle to trust any single signal. They don't know which version of the booth to believe.

So they stay cautious.

5. Messaging Inconsistency

Messaging includes signage, tags, tone, and implied promises.

> Handwritten signs mixed with polished branding
> Tags that explain some items but not others
> Value statements that shift tone booth to booth

Messaging inconsistency doesn't annoy buyers.

It unsettles them.
It suggests the booth is still negotiating with itself.
Buyers don't want to negotiate.
They want to choose.

Why Inconsistency Feels Harmless to Vendors

From the vendor's perspective, inconsistency often feels like adaptability.

You're responding to sales.
You're testing ideas.
You're making the booth more interesting.

Each change feels justified.

But buyers don't see the reasoning.
They only experience the outcome.

To them, inconsistency feels like instability.

And instability increases risk—even when prices are fair and inventory is strong.

The Compounding Effect

Inconsistency is not additive.
It's multiplicative.

One inconsistency makes a booth slightly harder to read.
Five inconsistencies make it exhausting.

Buyers don't consciously count them.
They just feel the weight.

And when the weight crosses a threshold, the buyer's brain chooses the safest available option:

Leave without deciding.

This is why vendors often feel blindsided.

> They didn't do anything "wrong."
> They didn't make a big mistake.
> They didn't break the booth.

They just let small mismatches accumulate.

Why Rearranging Doesn't Fix Inconsistency

Rearranging moves inconsistencies around.
It doesn't remove them.

> The same pricing logic exists.
> The same category collisions remain.
> The same quality variance persists.

The booth looks different—but it doesn't read easier.

That's why rearranging creates temporary relief followed by the same stall.

Novelty masks inconsistency briefly.
Trust does not.

The Tax You Don't See Until It's Gone

Inconsistency doesn't shut a booth down.
It taxes it.

> Each decision costs a little more.
> Each sale requires a little more luck.
> Each slow period feels heavier.

Over time, momentum weakens—not because the booth is bad, but because it's unreliable.

Buyers don't punish inconsistency.
They avoid it.

And avoidance looks exactly like "people just browsing."

The Core Truth

Buyers don't need perfection.
They need coherence.

>They will forgive small flaws.
>They will tolerate limits.
>They will accept prices.

What they won't do is spend energy decoding a booth that can't decide what it is.

Consistency doesn't make a booth boring.
It makes it readable.

And readable booths convert.

How Experienced Vendors Accidentally Break Trust

The irony of experience is that it often creates the very problems it's meant to prevent.

Experienced vendors don't lack skill. They don't lack knowledge. They don't lack effort. In most cases, they have better sourcing, stronger instincts, and a clearer sense of quality than newer sellers.

And yet—this is where trust most often erodes.

Not because experienced vendors make worse decisions, but because they make *more* of them.

Experience expands range. And range, when left unmanaged, creates inconsistency.

The Confidence Drift

As vendors gain experience, confidence grows. That confidence is earned—and deserved. But confidence also reduces friction, and friction is often what prevents overextension.

Experienced vendors feel comfortable bending rules because they've "seen what works."

They price some items emotionally.
They experiment without isolating variables.
They mix categories because they trust their eye.
They make exceptions because they've earned them.

Each exception feels reasonable.

But buyers don't see exceptions.
They see pattern breaks.

And pattern breaks introduce risk.

Over-Rotating Instead of Refining

New vendors under-rotate because they're afraid to change.
Experienced vendors over-rotate because they're afraid to
stagnate.

Inventory cycles too quickly.
Displays change without purpose.
Categories drift subtly week to week.

Buyers don't experience this as freshness.
They experience it as instability.

When nothing stays consistent long enough to be trusted, buyers
stop forming expectations. And when expectations disappear, so
does confidence.

Chasing Signals Instead of Patterns

Experienced vendors notice everything.

A comment.
A sale.
A slow afternoon.

The danger is mistaking signals for patterns.

One good sale leads to expansion.
One slow week leads to doubt.
One compliment leads to overemphasis.

Instead of responding to sustained behavior, the booth starts responding to moments.

Buyers don't reward responsiveness to noise.
They reward consistency to patterns.

Emotional Pricing Disguised as Strategy

Experience makes vendors acutely aware of effort.

> Time spent sourcing.
> Time spent restoring.
> Time spent waiting.

That awareness quietly creeps into pricing decisions.

Prices rise or soften based on emotion instead of structure.
Exceptions are made because "this one is different."
Confidence wavers after quiet periods.

Buyers don't know why prices changed.
They just feel that something shifted.

And unexplained shifts feel risky.

Mixing Sourcing Standards

Experienced vendors often source from multiple channels.

> Estate sales.
> Auctions.
> Private sellers.
> Wholesale.
> Handmade.

This diversity can be powerful—or destabilizing.

When sourcing standards mix without structure, quality variance creeps in. Buyers sense that some items are chosen carefully while others are tolerated.

They don't fault the booth.
They question its reliability.

Rearranging as Reassurance

When experienced vendors feel uncertainty, they move things.

> They know how to style.
> They know how to improve flow.
> They know how to refresh visuals.

> Rearranging feels like control.

But rearranging without addressing inconsistency just relocates it. The booth looks active—but trust doesn't rebuild.

Buyers don't respond to motion.
They respond to coherence.

Why Experience Makes This Hard to See

Experience creates familiarity.

Familiarity blinds.

Vendors stop seeing the booth as a buyer would. They remember why everything is there. They understand the logic behind every decision. That internal context replaces external clarity.

Buyers don't have that context.

They only see the surface.

And trust is built on what's visible—not what's intended.

The Uncomfortable Truth

Most experienced vendors don't lose trust because they stopped caring.

They lose it because they started trusting themselves more than the system.

Experience is powerful—but only when it's constrained.

Without constraints, experience creates drift.
Drift creates inconsistency.
Inconsistency taxes trust.

The Fix Isn't Less Experience

The solution is not to ignore instinct.
It's to discipline it.

Experience should narrow choices—not expand them.
It should refine standards—not loosen them.
It should reduce decisions—not multiply them.

The best-performing booths aren't run by the most creative vendors.

They're run by the most consistent ones.

Trust Compounds (Just Like Friction Does)

Trust doesn't arrive all at once.

It accumulates.

Quietly. Predictably. Almost invisibly.

And that's why vendors often underestimate its power.

Most vendors are trained—emotionally and practically—to look for spikes. Big days. Big weekends. Big reactions. They assume success should feel exciting, affirming, and obvious.

Trust doesn't feel like that.

Trust feels boring.

> It feels like fewer surprises.
> Fewer emotional swings.
> Fewer internal debates.

Which is exactly why it works.

How Buyers Learn to Trust a Booth

Buyers don't consciously decide to trust a booth.

They learn it through repetition.

> They notice that prices behave the same way each visit.
> They notice that categories don't drift.
> They notice that quality holds.
> They notice that decisions feel easier here than elsewhere.
> Nothing dramatic happens.
> Nothing flashy announces itself.

But over time, a subtle shift occurs.

The buyer stops re-evaluating the booth.

> They no longer ask:
> "Is this place worth my time?"
> "Is this priced fairly?"
> "Should I wait?"

They assume the answers.

And assumption is the most powerful form of trust.

Why Trust Speeds Decisions

When trust exists, buyers don't need to protect themselves.

> They don't scan for hidden catches.
> They don't hedge with delay.
> They don't overthink.

They choose.

This is why trusted booths often sell at higher price points with less resistance. Buyers aren't paying more because they're excited. They're paying more because they feel safe deciding.

Safety removes friction.
Friction removal increases velocity.

Velocity—not novelty—is what sustains momentum.

Why Friction Compounds Faster Than Trust

Trust builds slowly.
Friction builds instantly.

> One confusing price.
> One mismatched display.
> One unexplained shift.

Those moments undo weeks of consistency.

This asymmetry is frustrating—but it's reality.

Trust must be protected deliberately because it erodes effortlessly.

That's why vendors who rely on excitement struggle long-term. Excitement requires constant input. Trust requires maintenance—but far less energy.

Why "Boring" Booths Win

The highest-performing booths often look uneventful from the inside.

> Inventory turns predictably.
> Restocking feels routine.
> Layout rarely changes.
> Pricing doesn't swing.

To the vendor, it can feel stagnant.

To buyers, it feels reliable.

Reliable booths become mental anchors. Buyers remember them without effort. They return without intention. They recommend them casually.

Not because they're impressed—
But because they're comfortable.

Comfort shortens the distance between browsing and buying.

The Hidden Advantage of Trust

Trust reduces emotional labor for the vendor too.

When buyers trust the booth:

- You stop justifying prices
- You stop chasing reactions
- You stop reacting to every slow period

Decisions feel calmer because the system is doing the work.

Trust shifts effort from reaction to maintenance.
From panic to stewardship.

That's where sustainability lives.

Trust Is the Only Advantage That Scales
Trends fade.
Inventory changes.
Markets shift.

Trust compounds regardless.

It survives slow seasons.
It cushions bad months.
It stabilizes growth.

And once it exists, it's surprisingly resilient—as long as it's respected.

That's why trust is the multiplier.

Everything else only works when it's present.

The Trust Checklist (Without Turning It Into Rules)
Trust is fragile—but it doesn't require perfection.

What it requires is protection.

Most vendors assume protecting trust means adding more effort: more signs, more explanation, more adjustments. In reality, trust is preserved by *removing uncertainty*, not adding activity.

This is where a checklist helps—not as a set of rigid rules, but as a recurring filter. Something you can quietly run in your head before changes compound into drift.

These questions are not about optimizing.
They're about safeguarding clarity.

1. Does My Booth Tell One Story—or Several?

Not one style.
Not one category.

One *logic*.

A buyer should be able to understand what kind of booth this is within seconds. If the booth requires interpretation—if buyers have to reconcile multiple identities at once—trust weakens.

If you can't explain your booth's role in a single sentence, buyers can't either.

2. Do Prices Behave the Same Way Everywhere?

Prices don't need to be uniform.
They need to be consistent.

Similar items should follow similar logic.
Price jumps should feel intentional, not arbitrary.
Nothing should feel like it was priced emotionally last week.

Buyers don't memorize prices.
They remember patterns.

Patterns create safety.

3. Does Presentation Match Expectation?

Higher prices demand stronger structure.
Lower prices tolerate looseness.

When presentation and pricing disagree, buyers feel it instantly.
They may not articulate why—but they hesitate.

Ask yourself:
If someone saw this display without a price tag, would the price
feel reasonable once revealed?

If not, trust is being taxed.

4. Is Anything Here Asking Buyers to "Figure It Out"?

Every time a buyer has to decode something, trust takes a hit.

> What category is this?
> Why is this priced higher?
> Is this special—or just here?

Buyers don't want explanations.
They want reassurance.

If something requires justification, it's not ready.

5. Would This Booth Still Make Sense Next Month?

This is one of the most revealing questions.

Trust is built on predictability—not sameness, but continuity.
Buyers return expecting the booth to feel familiar, even if
inventory changes.

If the booth feels like an experiment in progress, buyers don't
commit. They wait.

Waiting is the opposite of trust.

6. Am I Protecting Clarity—or Chasing Reaction?

This question separates maintenance from sabotage.

If a change is being made to:

- Fix a clear pattern
- Support proven movement
- Reduce friction

It likely protects trust.

If a change is being made to:

- Fight a slow week
- Respond to a comment
- Inject excitement

It probably erodes it.

The Point of the Checklist

This checklist isn't about control.
It's about restraint.

It exists to catch drift early—before it becomes expensive, emotional, or invisible.

Trust doesn't require constant improvement.
It requires consistency that's defended.

When trust is protected, everything else becomes easier:

> Pricing feels steadier.
> Inventory decisions calm down.
> Momentum stops feeling fragile.

And that's when the booth stops demanding attention—and starts returning it.

Chapter Takeaway

Trust is not a bonus.
It's the multiplier.

Every inconsistency taxes it.
Every coherent decision reinforces it.

Once trust is established, buyers don't re-evaluate your booth every visit.
They accept it.

And acceptance is what turns browsing into buying—again and again

Control the Variable or the Booth Will Control You

When Everything Feels Right but Nothing Moves

There is a moment most vendors aren't prepared for.

It doesn't happen when the booth is broken.
It doesn't happen when sales are terrible.
It happens **after** you fix the obvious problems.

Pricing makes sense now.
The booth feels coherent.
Buyers linger longer.
Nothing feels *wrong* anymore.

And yet—sales don't rise the way you expect them to.

This moment is uniquely frustrating because it violates logic. The effort is there. The structure is there. The booth no longer feels chaotic or confused. By every visible metric, progress should follow.

When it doesn't, vendors often assume one of two things:

Either the market is worse than they thought,
or something unseen is still broken.

Neither conclusion is usually correct.

What's actually happening is quieter—and more dangerous.

You've entered a phase where **results are no longer being blocked**, but they're also no longer being interpreted correctly.

At this stage, most booths don't suffer from friction.
They suffer from **signal loss**.

The Illusion of "It Should Be Working by Now"

Once pricing friction is removed and trust begins to form, vendors expect momentum to arrive naturally. They assume stability should immediately translate into acceleration.

123

When it doesn't, impatience creeps in.

The booth feels close.
So close that waiting feels irresponsible.

Small changes start to feel justified again:

> Maybe the layout needs refreshing
> Maybe this category needs more emphasis
> Maybe prices need a little push
> Maybe signage needs more explanation

None of these ideas are unreasonable on their own.

The problem is what happens next.

When Progress Becomes Unreadable

At this stage, vendors often make **multiple adjustments in rapid succession**, all in the name of "fine-tuning."

> Inventory shifts.
> Displays move.
> Prices adjust.
> Messaging evolves.

Each change feels like refinement.

But refinement only works when feedback is clear.

When too many variables move at once, the booth stops giving usable information. Sales become impossible to interpret. Slow days feel personal. Good days feel accidental.

You're no longer learning from the booth.

You're reacting to it.

This is the moment when vendors say things like:

> "I don't know what's working anymore."
> "I feel like I'm always adjusting."
> "I'm doing everything right, but it's still unpredictable."

That unpredictability isn't coming from the market.

It's coming from **loss of control over the system.**

Why This Phase Feels Worse Than the Struggle Phase

Struggling booths are frustrating—but they're understandable. There's something obvious to fix. A clear problem to solve.

This phase is harder because nothing is clearly broken.

The booth feels *almost* stable.
The results feel *almost* reliable.

That "almost" creates anxiety.

So vendors try to force clarity by changing things—hoping the next adjustment will unlock momentum.

Instead, they blur it further.

Buyers Feel This Before Vendors Do

Buyers don't analyze changes the way vendors do.

They don't track what moved or what changed.
They just sense whether the booth feels settled.

When too many elements shift at once, buyers don't feel excitement.

They feel uncertainty.

Uncertainty doesn't trigger rejection.
It triggers delay.

And delay looks exactly like:

- Browsing without buying
- Interest without commitment
- Compliments without conversion

The booth isn't untrustworthy anymore.
It's just no longer *readable*.

The Real Problem Isn't Effort
At this point, effort is rarely the issue.

The problem is that **the booth is doing too much at once**—and teaching you nothing in return.

> You can't tell which decisions helped.
> You can't tell which hurt.
> You can't tell what to repeat.

Without control, every outcome feels ambiguous.

And ambiguity is where confidence dies—both for the vendor and the buyer.

What This Chapter Is About
This chapter is not about slowing down.

It's about **regaining control.**

> Control over what changes.
> Control over what stays fixed.
> Control over what signals you're actually measuring.

Because once a booth becomes stable and trusted, the fastest way to sabotage it isn't bad decisions.

It's **too many decisions at the same time.**

And until that's corrected, momentum will always feel fragile—no matter how good the booth becomes.

The Booth Is a System, Not a Collection of Ideas
One of the most damaging myths in booth selling is the idea that success comes from having *better ideas.*

> Better themes.
> Better displays.
> Better concepts.
> Better instincts.

This belief feels natural because booths are visual, creative spaces. Vendors are encouraged—explicitly or implicitly—to treat them as evolving expressions of taste, personality, and inspiration.

That mindset works early.

But once a booth reaches stability, that same mindset becomes the liability.

Because buyers don't respond to ideas.

They respond to **systems**.

Why Systems Convert and Ideas Don't

An idea is isolated.

A system is repeatable.

Ideas attract attention.
Systems create confidence.

Buyers don't need novelty to decide. They need reliability. They need to feel that what they're seeing is part of a larger logic—one that will still make sense after the moment passes.

> A booth built on ideas asks the buyer to interpret.
> A booth built on systems allows the buyer to choose.

That distinction matters more than most vendors realize.

When a booth behaves like a system, buyers unconsciously learn how to interact with it. They understand where to look, what to expect, and how decisions are supposed to work.

When a booth behaves like a collection of ideas, buyers have to orient themselves every time.

Orientation costs energy.
Energy loss creates hesitation.

The Vendor's Perspective vs. the Buyer's Reality

From inside the booth, ideas feel exciting.

You know why something was added.
You remember what inspired a change.
You understand the logic behind the display.

From the buyer's perspective, none of that context exists.

They don't see evolution.
They see **behavior**.

And behavior is what builds—or breaks—trust.

If the booth behaves predictably, buyers relax.
If the booth behaves erratically, buyers stay cautious.

It doesn't matter how good the ideas are.
What matters is whether they align into something readable.

Systems Reduce Decision Cost

A system does something crucial:

It limits variability.

That limitation isn't restrictive—it's protective.

When buyers recognize patterns, they stop spending mental energy decoding the space. They don't ask themselves what kind of booth this is or how pricing works here. They already know.

That familiarity creates ease.

Ease shortens the distance between interest and commitment.

This is why system-driven booths often outperform more "creative" ones. They don't feel smarter. They feel safer.

Why Experienced Vendors Resist Systems

Ironically, experienced vendors are the ones most likely to resist system thinking.

They trust their eye.
They trust their instincts.
They trust their ability to adapt.

And those strengths are real.

But instincts are situational.
Systems are durable.

When a booth relies on instinct alone, every decision becomes a fresh judgment call. Over time, those calls stack up—and variability creeps in.

The booth starts behaving differently week to week, even if no single change feels dramatic.

Buyers don't experience that as growth.
They experience it as inconsistency.

Systems Don't Eliminate Creativity—They Channel It

A system does not mean uniformity.
It does not mean stagnation.
It does not mean suppressing instinct.

It means creativity operates **within boundaries**.

Those boundaries ensure that new ideas:

- Fit the booth's logic
- Reinforce existing patterns
- Strengthen buyer confidence instead of testing it

Without boundaries, creativity becomes noise.

With boundaries, creativity becomes refinement.

The Shift That Changes Everything

The moment a vendor stops asking:
"What new idea can I try?"

And starts asking:
"What system am I protecting?"

Everything changes.

Decisions become calmer.
Results become clearer.
Confidence stops swinging with each sale—or lack of one.

The booth stops being a reflection of mood, momentum, or anxiety.

It becomes a stable environment buyers can rely on.

And reliability—not brilliance—is what converts consistently.

Too Many Variables Kill Feedback

Most vendors believe they're "testing" when they change things in their booth.

In reality, they're erasing their own feedback.

> Testing requires control.
> Control requires limits.
> And limits are exactly what most vendors abandon once they feel pressure to improve.

When results don't move the way a vendor expects, the instinct is to *do more*. More adjustments. More changes. More experimentation. The belief is that activity will reveal the answer.

Instead, it removes it.

Why Feedback Is the Only Thing That Actually Matters

A booth teaches you through contrast.

> You make a change.
> You observe a result.
> You learn.

That learning only works if the system remains stable enough to isolate cause and effect.

When multiple elements shift at once, the booth stops communicating. Sales rise or fall, but there's no signal—only noise.

> Was it the price?
> The display?

The category?
The timing?
The weather?
The weekend?

You can't know.

So the next change is made blind.

The Most Common Variable Pileups

Most vendors don't make *one* change.

They make five.

> A category gets expanded.
> Prices adjust "slightly."
> Inventory turns over.
> Layout shifts.
> Signage evolves.

Each change feels incremental.

Together, they destroy interpretability.

Instead of learning, the vendor is guessing—just with more steps.

Why This Happens Right After Progress

This behavior usually appears **after** a booth improves.

Once friction is reduced and trust begins forming, vendors expect movement. When it doesn't arrive immediately, impatience kicks in.

The booth feels close enough that waiting feels like failure.

So the vendor starts tweaking.

But tweaking isn't refinement when it's uncontrolled.

It's interference.

Buyers Experience This as Instability

Buyers don't analyze variables. They sense pattern integrity.

When too many elements shift, buyers don't think:
"They're testing something."

They think:
"This place feels unsettled."

Unsettled environments trigger caution.

Caution delays decisions.

Delayed decisions are indistinguishable from disinterest at the register—but they're not the same thing.

Why Rearranging Is the Most Dangerous Change

Rearranging feels productive because it's visible.

> It creates motion.
> It creates novelty.
> It creates the illusion of improvement.

But rearranging changes *everything* at once.

> Item relationships.
> Visual hierarchy.
> Flow.
> Context.

When you rearrange while also changing inventory or pricing, you've altered so many variables that any result becomes meaningless.

> If sales rise, you won't know why.
> If they fall, you'll assume something is wrong.

Either way, you learn nothing.

The Emotional Cost of Uncontrolled Change

When feedback disappears, confidence erodes.

Good days feel accidental.
Bad days feel personal.
Every result invites reinterpretation.

This is how vendors end up emotionally exhausted by booths that are objectively functional.

They aren't failing.
They're just operating without clarity.

And clarity is what sustains momentum.

Why More Experience Makes This Worse

Experienced vendors change faster.

They recognize options.
They notice possibilities.
They trust their instincts.

That speed is an advantage—until it overwhelms the system.

The more skilled the vendor, the easier it is to over-adjust.

Skill without constraint doesn't produce mastery.

It produces chaos with better aesthetics.

What Controlled Testing Actually Looks Like

Real testing is boring.

One change.
One variable.
One outcome.

Everything else stays fixed long enough to be measured.

That patience feels uncomfortable at first—especially for vendors used to "working the booth."

But it's the only way the booth teaches you anything useful.

Without control, the booth becomes a mirror for anxiety.

With control, it becomes a source of insight.

The Hard Truth
If you can't explain *why* something worked, you didn't learn anything.

And if you didn't learn anything, you can't repeat it.

Too many variables don't create opportunity.

They erase it.

The Discipline of Changing One Thing at a Time
The solution to variable overload isn't creativity.

It's restraint.

This is where most vendors struggle—not because they don't understand the logic, but because the discipline feels unnatural. Changing one thing at a time feels slow. Passive. Almost negligent.

But discipline is what turns movement into knowledge.

Why Restraint Feels So Uncomfortable
Vendors are conditioned to equate activity with progress.

>   If sales dip, *do something*.
>   If momentum slows, *adjust something*.
>   If uncertainty creeps in, *move something*.

Restraint feels like surrender.

But restraint isn't inaction.
It's **controlled action**.

It's the decision to protect the signal long enough to understand it.

What "One Change" Actually Means

Changing one thing doesn't mean touching only one item.

It means changing **one variable class**.

Examples:

- Pricing logic across a category
- Presentation style for a defined area
- Inventory depth within a single type
- Signage clarity for one message

Everything else stays fixed.

> Not forever.
> Long enough to be read.

That time horizon is longer than most vendors want—but shorter than the cost of confusion.

The Time Buyers Need to Respond

Buyers don't react instantly to change.

They need repetition.

They need to encounter the booth multiple times under the same conditions before behavior shifts. That takes time—often weeks, not days.

If changes reset before buyers can absorb them, results will always feel muted.

You didn't fail.
You just didn't let the system speak.

Why Experienced Vendors Break This Rule First

Experience accelerates decision-making.

That speed becomes a liability here.

Experienced vendors see improvements they *could* make—and feel compelled to act on them. They confuse potential with urgency.

The result is constant adjustment without resolution.

Restraint feels like underuse of skill.
In reality, it's mastery.

Stability Is What Allows Precision
Precision only works in stable environments.

When everything else is fixed, small changes become visible. Their impact becomes obvious. Success stops feeling mysterious.

You don't wonder what worked.
You know.

That knowledge builds confidence that doesn't depend on today's sales.

Why "Letting It Sit" Is an Advanced Skill
Letting a booth sit doesn't mean ignoring it.

It means observing without interfering.

> You're watching patterns form.
> You're gathering data.
> You're learning how buyers actually behave—not how you hope they will.

That patience is rare.
And it's why so few booths ever feel truly predictable.

The Compounding Benefit of Discipline
Once discipline becomes habit, everything changes.

Adjustments become intentional.
Anxiety drops.
Momentum stabilizes.

The booth stops demanding constant attention.

Not because it's static—
But because it's understood.

How Control Creates Confidence (For You and the Buyer)
Confidence in a booth doesn't come from sales.

Sales fluctuate.
Traffic shifts.
Seasons change.

If confidence depended on outcomes alone, it would never stabilize.

Real confidence comes from **understanding**.

When you can explain why something is happening, uncertainty loses its power. Good days feel earned. Slow days feel contextual. Decisions stop feeling reactive.

Control creates that understanding.

Why Vendors Lose Confidence Even When Sales Improve
One of the strangest patterns in booth selling is that confidence often *drops* right after progress.

Sales improve—but feel fragile.
Momentum appears—but feels temporary.
Every dip triggers concern.

This happens when improvements aren't understood.

If you don't know *what* caused growth, you can't trust it. You brace for reversal. You stay on edge.

Control replaces that anxiety with clarity.

The Vendor's Side: Calm Through Causality

When variables are controlled, results become traceable.

You know:

- What you changed
- Why you changed it
- What effect it had

That knowledge stabilizes emotion.

> You stop chasing reassurance.
> You stop overcorrecting.
> You stop interpreting every slow day as failure.

The booth becomes a system you manage—not a mood you react to.

The Buyer's Side: Confidence Through Consistency

Buyers don't see your process—but they feel its effects.

Controlled booths behave predictably.
Predictability signals safety.
Safety encourages commitment.

When buyers encounter the same logic repeatedly:

- Prices behave the same
- Categories stay consistent
- Presentation feels familiar

They relax.

Relaxed buyers decide faster.

Why Control Strengthens Trust Instead of Limiting It

Some vendors fear that control makes a booth rigid.

In reality, it makes it **readable**.

> Buyers don't want surprise rules.
> They want stable expectations.

Control ensures that creativity doesn't undermine clarity. It keeps trust intact while allowing evolution to happen gradually—without shocking the system.

Confidence Changes Vendor Behavior

When confidence stabilizes, behavior changes naturally.

> You stop rearranging for reassurance.
> You stop explaining prices.
> You stop chasing reaction.

That restraint reinforces trust.

Buyers sense calm.
Calm signals authority.
Authority invites belief.

The Quiet Loop That Sustains Momentum

Control creates understanding.
Understanding creates confidence.
Confidence reinforces consistency.
Consistency strengthens trust.

This loop sustains momentum without constant effort.

> The booth stops feeling fragile.
> You stop feeling defensive.
> Buyers stop hesitating.

Not because everything is perfect—
But because everything makes sense.

The Variable Control Filter

Control doesn't come from rules.

Rules are brittle. They invite rebellion, shortcuts, and rational exceptions. What actually protects a booth is a **filter**—a quiet decision screen that slows you down just enough to preserve clarity.

Before any change is made, this filter asks a few simple questions.

Not to stop progress.
To protect understanding.

1. What Exactly Is Changing?

Not "the booth."
Not "the vibe."
Not "a refresh."

One thing.

A pricing rule.
A category depth.
A display structure.
A message being communicated.

If you can't name the variable cleanly, it's not controlled.

2. Why Is It Changing *Now*?

There are only a few valid reasons to change something:

A clear pattern emerged
A repeated friction point appeared
A proven category needs support

If the reason is:

"I'm nervous,"
"I'm bored,"
"It's been slow,"

That's not strategy.
That's anxiety asking for motion.

Motion doesn't equal progress.

3. What Outcome Am I Measuring?

Every controlled change has a measurable intent.

> More units moved
> Faster decision-making
> Higher average ticket
> Less buyer hesitation

If success can't be described in advance, it can't be recognized afterward.

You're not testing.
You're hoping.

4. What Is *Not* Changing Right Now?

This is the most important question—and the one most vendors skip.

Control only exists when something stays fixed.

> Pricing stays the same
> Layout stays the same
> Category mix stays the same

Whatever isn't changing becomes the reference point.

Without a reference point, results float.
Floating results destroy confidence.

5. How Long Will I Let This Run?

Controlled change requires patience.

Not infinite patience.
Defined patience.

Two weeks.
One month.
A full inventory cycle.

If you don't set a time horizon, emotion will reset the system before learning happens.

Why This Filter Works

This filter doesn't slow growth.

It **protects insight**.

It turns change into information instead of noise.
It prevents emotional overcorrection.
It keeps trust intact—both yours and the buyer's.

Most importantly, it ensures that when something works, you know *why*.

And when something doesn't, you know *what to fix*.

Chapter Takeaway

Momentum doesn't disappear because booths stop working.

It disappears because vendors lose control of what's changing.

Once pricing is clear and trust is established, the greatest threat to progress isn't the market—it's uncontrolled motion. Too many decisions. Too many variables. Too much activity masking a lack of clarity.

Control doesn't mean doing less.

It means changing with intent.
Observing with patience.
Protecting the signal.

When you control the variables, the booth starts teaching you again.

And when the booth teaches you, progress stops feeling fragile.

It becomes repeatable.

That's when momentum stops needing constant effort—and starts sustaining itself.

Scaling Before You're Ready and Why It Breaks Momentum

The most dangerous moment in a booth's life is not failure.

It's improvement.

Failure is loud. It demands attention. It forces restraint. Vendors who are struggling don't debate what to do next—they narrow their focus, slow down, and work on what's obviously broken. There is clarity in struggle, even when it's uncomfortable.

Improvement does the opposite.

When pricing finally settles, when buyers hesitate less, when inventory begins to move with some predictability, the booth stops fighting you. Decisions feel lighter. Restocking feels purposeful instead of desperate. You no longer feel like every visit requires emotional armor, or that every quiet day carries a hidden threat.

That calm is earned.

But it creates a new kind of risk.

Because the moment something starts working, the pressure to capitalize appears. Not loudly. Quietly. Reasonably. It shows up as a thought that feels responsible rather than reckless.

The Relief That Masquerades as Readiness

After a long stretch of friction—pricing doubt, inconsistent sales, constant second-guessing—stability feels like progress in its purest form.

> The booth feels quieter.
> You're not reacting every day.
> Nothing feels on fire.

That relief is powerful. It brings a sense of control that may have been missing for a long time.

And it's exactly why so many vendors misread it.

Relief feels like capacity.
Calm feels like margin.
Stability feels like permission.

But relief is not proof that the system can carry more weight. It's only proof that the system is no longer overloaded *at its current size*. It says nothing about how that system will behave under added pressure.

That distinction is subtle—and costly when missed.

The Emotional Timeline Vendors Rarely Notice
For most vendors, this phase unfolds quietly:

First, friction is removed.
Then sales stabilize.
Then confidence returns.

And then comparison creeps in.

You notice vendors expanding.
You notice larger booths.
You notice people "doing more."

Suddenly, staying the same feels like stagnation. Even if nothing is broken, growth starts to feel overdue. Holding steady feels like hesitation instead of discipline. Inaction starts to feel irresponsible—like you're failing to act on an opportunity you worked hard to earn.

So expansion becomes framed as the next logical step—not because the booth demands it, but because standing still feels uncomfortable.

This is how readiness gets replaced by urgency.

Why Confidence Accelerates the Wrong Decisions
Improvement creates confidence, and confidence lowers friction.

That's normally a good thing. Lower friction is what allows momentum to build in the first place.

But lower friction also means fewer internal checks. Vendors start trusting instinct again—pricing instinct, sourcing instinct, expansion instinct—without stopping to ask whether the system has actually been tested under pressure.

Confidence answers the question:
"Can I do this?"

Capacity answers a different one:
"Can I keep doing this when it's harder, slower, or less rewarding?"

Most vendors never stop to ask the second question—because confidence feels like the answer already exists.

Fragile Momentum Doesn't Announce Itself

At this stage, momentum exists—but it's conditional.

> It works because pricing is contained.
> Inventory is controlled.
> Decisions are limited.
> Attention is focused.

Remove those constraints too quickly and momentum doesn't slow down.

It fractures.

But that fracture doesn't show up immediately in sales. It shows up internally—through decision fatigue, restock stress, and subtle loss of clarity. The booth begins to feel heavier again, even if the numbers haven't caught up yet.

By the time sales reflect the damage, the system has already shifted.

Why Vendors Don't See the Reset Coming

Premature scaling doesn't look like a mistake at first.

Sales may even rise.
The booth may look impressive.
Validation may increase.

That early feedback masks the strain underneath. The system is being asked to perform beyond what it has proven it can sustain—but there's no warning light for that. No dashboard alert. No obvious failure.

Just a gradual return of weight.

This chapter is not about slowing ambition.

It's about protecting momentum at the moment it's most vulnerable.

Because scaling is not a reward for improvement.

It's a stress test.

And failing that test doesn't mean you weren't capable—it means the system wasn't ready to be trusted with more.

More Space, More Inventory, More Problems
Expansion feels logical.

If a booth is working, giving it more space should make it work better. If inventory moves, adding more should increase sales. If buyers respond well, offering more options should raise totals.

That logic feels so obvious that most vendors never stop to question it.

And that's exactly why it causes so much damage.

Why Expansion Starts to Feel "Responsible"
Once a booth stabilizes, standing still starts to feel uncomfortable.

Sales are steadier.
Pricing finally makes sense.
The booth no longer feels fragile or unpredictable.

At that point, *not* expanding begins to feel like hesitation.
Vendors worry that if they don't act, they're wasting momentum.
Holding the same footprint starts to feel like fear instead of discipline.

Expansion gets reframed as the responsible choice.

> *"If this works, I should lean into it."*
> *"If demand exists, I should support it."*
> *"If I don't grow now, I'll miss my window."*

None of those thoughts are reckless.

They're premature.

Scaling Doesn't Add Strength — It Exposes Structure

Expansion does not create capacity.

It exposes whether capacity already exists.

In a small booth, inconsistencies can hide. Pricing logic doesn't get tested across as many items. Category boundaries don't have to be perfectly defined. Quality variation can be tolerated because it isn't amplified.

When space increases, those protections disappear.

Pricing logic has to stretch across more inventory.
Category discipline has to hold across more surface area.
Presentation standards have to be maintained without exception.

Anything that isn't structurally sound becomes visible.

The booth doesn't become worse.

It becomes louder.

The Square Footage Illusion

Many vendors believe more space will solve existing bottlenecks.

They imagine:

- Better flow

- Cleaner displays

- Inventory finally having room to breathe

What actually happens is more complicated.

New space creates areas that don't quite belong to anything yet. Dead zones appear. Walls get filled simply because empty space feels wasteful. Displays stretch beyond what inventory can support, forcing filler into places it doesn't belong.

Space introduces pressure.

Pressure introduces compromise.

To buyers, neither empty space nor overfilled space feels neutral. Both signal instability—either uncertainty or excess.

The "I Have to Fill It Now" Problem
New square footage creates urgency that didn't exist before.

Inventory that once felt sufficient now feels thin. Restocking shifts from intentional to reactive. Sourcing becomes driven by the need to occupy space rather than support demand.

Vendors start buying *to justify the booth* instead of serving the buyer.

That shift doesn't feel reckless in the moment. It feels necessary.

But it's the moment discipline quietly breaks.

Inventory Expansion Is Not a Neutral Act
Inventory feels productive because it's tangible.

> You can see it.
> You can touch it.
> You can justify it as effort.

But inventory carries weight:

- Cash stays tied up longer
- Turn speed slows
- Visual clarity erodes
- Restocking pressure increases

More inventory does not automatically create more sales.

It creates more responsibility.

And when responsibility grows faster than systems, momentum stalls instead of accelerates.

Category Creep Is How Focus Disappears

As booths grow, categories rarely expand cleanly.

A strong category invites adjacent items.
A related piece sneaks in.
A "temporary experiment" becomes permanent.

Each addition feels reasonable.
None feel dangerous.

But together, they erase specialization.

Buyers stop understanding what the booth is *about*. The mental shortcut they once had disappears.

Specialization builds trust.
Expansion without focus erodes it.

Why Bigger Booths Fail Faster

This is the part vendors rarely expect.

Larger booths don't fail slowly.

They fail loudly.

Costs rise immediately. Weak categories expose themselves. Maintenance demands multiply. There's less margin for uncertainty and less room to hide mistakes.

Vendors often interpret this as market resistance or personal failure.

It's neither.

It's structural overload.

Expansion Is an Audit, Not a Solution

Expansion doesn't fix friction.

It audits whether friction was actually removed.

If clarity, pricing logic, and trust can't survive more space, they weren't stable—they were merely contained.

More space doesn't create opportunity.

It tests whether opportunity was real.

Capacity Is the Real Limiter (Not Demand)

Most vendors believe growth stops because demand runs out.

In practice, growth almost always stops because **capacity does**.

Demand is loud. It shows up as foot traffic, interest, compliments, and sales spikes. Capacity is quiet. It doesn't announce itself. It simply tightens until the booth starts feeling heavy again.

That heaviness is the first real signal vendors miss.

Why Demand Gets the Blame

Demand is easier to point at.

When sales slow, it's comforting to believe buyers disappeared, trends shifted, or the market changed. Those explanations feel external and uncontrollable—which makes them emotionally safer.

Capacity failure feels personal.

It suggests that the system reached its limit, not that opportunity vanished. That implication makes vendors uncomfortable, so it's often ignored until damage appears elsewhere.

How Capacity Actually Fails (In Real Time)

Capacity failure rarely looks dramatic at first.

It unfolds quietly:

> The booth expands.
> Inventory increases.
> Restocking takes longer.

Then small things slip.

> Pricing discipline softens.
> Standards relax.
> Decisions get deferred.
> Maintenance feels rushed instead of routine.

Nothing breaks all at once.

The booth just becomes harder to maintain.

That difficulty gets misinterpreted as workload, not warning.

The Four Capacities That Collapse First

Capacity is not a single constraint. It's a system of limits that fail together when pushed too far.

1. Physical Capacity

Physical capacity isn't about square footage.

It's about **maintainable structure.**

As booths grow, presentation standards become harder to hold consistently. Visual hierarchy weakens. Dead zones form where nothing quite belongs. Displays stretch beyond what inventory can support.

Buyers feel this as disorganization—even when nothing looks "wrong" on paper.

Space only helps if it can be maintained at the same standard.

2. Financial Capacity

Expansion ties up cash faster than most vendors expect.

More inventory means:

- Longer recovery time
- Higher exposure to slow movers
- Less flexibility during slow months

Even profitable booths can become fragile when too much capital is immobilized.

Growth that stresses cash flow is not growth.

It's leverage without margin.

3. Time & Restock Capacity

Every additional square foot adds work.

> More cleaning.
> More monitoring.
> More replacement.
> More decisions.

If restocking begins to feel rushed, reactive, or emotionally loaded, capacity has already been exceeded.

Time does not scale just because ambition does.

4. Emotional & Decision Capacity

This is the capacity vendors underestimate most—and pay for most often.

Every booth decision costs mental energy.
Every slow day costs emotional energy.

As booths grow, decision volume increases:
> What to replace
> What to move
> What to discount
> What to explain

When decision fatigue sets in, discipline erodes. Vendors stop managing systems and start reacting to pressure.

That's when inconsistency returns.

Why Capacity Failure Feels "Normal" at First

This is the most dangerous part.

Capacity failure doesn't feel like collapse.

It feels like:
> *"I'm just busy."*
> *"I just need to catch up."*
> *"This is temporary."*

So vendors push harder.

Effort masks the real problem until trust, clarity, and control start slipping quietly in the background.

By the time sales reflect the damage, momentum has already weakened.

Capacity Is the Governor on Growth

Demand invites growth.

Capacity determines whether growth survives.

Ignoring capacity doesn't increase opportunity—it increases stress.

True readiness means growth does not require shortcuts.

If expansion forces compromise, it wasn't earned.

The Quiet Signal of Sufficient Capacity

When capacity is sufficient:

- Growth feels boring
- Systems hold under pressure
- Decisions remain calm
- Slow periods don't trigger panic

If growth feels urgent, chaotic, or exhausting, capacity has already been exceeded—even if demand still exists.

Why Capacity Fails Before Demand Does

Buyers don't disappear overnight.

But vendors burn out quietly.

> They feel overwhelmed.
> They feel behind.
> They feel like the booth suddenly demands constant attention again.

That pressure leads to shortcuts.

Shortcuts lead to inconsistency.

Inconsistency resets trust.

The Illusion of "I'll Figure It Out"

Many vendors scale believing they'll adapt as they go.

Sometimes they do.

More often, they adapt by lowering standards:

- Accepting slower turns
- Tolerating weaker inventory
- Letting presentation slide
- Making emotional pricing decisions

The booth doesn't collapse immediately.

It degrades.

Capacity Is the Governor on Growth

Demand invites growth.
Capacity governs it.

Ignoring capacity doesn't increase opportunity.
It just increases stress.

True readiness isn't about wanting more.
It's about being able to handle more **without changing behavior**.

If expansion requires shortcuts, it wasn't earned.

The Quiet Signal of Readiness

When capacity is sufficient:

- Growth feels boring
- Systems hold under pressure
- Decision-making stays calm
- Restocking feels manageable

If growth feels urgent, chaotic, or exhausting, capacity has already been exceeded.

The Readiness Test Most Vendors Skip

Most vendors decide they're ready to grow based on feeling.

> Sales feel steadier.
> The booth feels calmer.
> Confidence is returning.

Those signals matter—but they're not enough.

Readiness isn't emotional.
It's operational.

And very few vendors actually test it before scaling.

The Question Vendors Avoid

Before expanding, there is one question that matters more than any other:

Can this booth run without my constant intervention?

Not neglect.
Not abandonment.

Consistency without pressure.

If the booth only works because you're constantly adjusting, expanding it will amplify stress—not results.

Test #1 — Can You Predict Sales Without Guessing?

You don't need perfect accuracy.

But you should be able to say:

> "This category will likely move X over the next month."
> "This price range turns steadily."
> "This section underperforms consistently."

If sales still feel random, scaling multiplies uncertainty.
Growth doesn't create clarity.
It requires it.

Test #2 — Can You Restock Without Stress?

Restocking should feel routine.

If it feels rushed, chaotic, or emotionally loaded, capacity has already been reached. More space will not fix that.

A scalable booth allows you to:

- Know what needs replacing
- Source deliberately
- Maintain quality without urgency

If restocking feels reactive, growth will magnify the problem.

Test #3 — Can You Explain *Why* Items Move?

This is the difference between luck and understanding.

If you can explain:

- Why certain items sell faster
- Why certain price points perform better
- Why certain categories underperform

You're ready to reinforce success.

If not, expansion turns guessing into investment risk.

Test #4 — Can the Booth Survive a Slow Month Without Panic?

Every booth has slow months.

Readiness shows in response.

If a slow period triggers:

- Heavy discounting
- Rapid rearranging
- Emotional sourcing
- Strategy abandonment

The system isn't stable yet.

Scaling during instability compounds damage.

Test #5 — Can You Change One Thing at a Time?

This is the final test—and the hardest.

If expansion forces you to:

- Change pricing
- Change layout
- Change categories
- Change sourcing
- Change messaging

All at once, you weren't ready.

True readiness allows growth **without changing behavior**.

Why Vendors Skip These Tests

Because they're uncomfortable.

>They slow momentum.
>They delay gratification.
>They force restraint when excitement is high.

But skipping them doesn't make growth faster.

It makes collapse faster.

The Hard Truth

Readiness doesn't feel exciting.

>It feels boring.
>Predictable.
>Under control.

If growth feels urgent, it's not ready.

If growth feels obvious, it probably is.

Why Scaling Too Early Resets the Clock

Premature scaling doesn't just slow a booth down.

It sends it backward.

Not visibly at first. Not dramatically. But structurally—where the damage actually matters.

This is why vendors often struggle to explain what went wrong. Nothing obviously failed. Sales may have even increased. Traffic might still look healthy. From the outside, the booth appears bigger, busier, more successful.

From the inside, it feels heavier.

And that heaviness is the reset.

Why Early Expansion Feels Like Regression

Vendors who scale too early often describe the same experience:

> "I was doing better before."
> "I don't understand why this feels harder now."
> "I fixed all of this already."

That confusion creates doubt—not just in the booth, but in the vendor's own judgment. Confidence that took months to rebuild suddenly feels fragile again.

This isn't because skill disappeared.

It's because the system lost protection.

Expansion Reintroduces Beginner Problems

Every booth starts its life fighting the same battles:

- Unclear pricing
- Mixed categories
- Visual overload
- Emotional decision-making
- Constant adjustment

Chapters 7–9 exist to remove those problems.

Scaling too early quietly brings them back.

Pricing logic stretches until it becomes inconsistent. Category boundaries soften. Presentation standards slip under maintenance pressure. Control erodes as decisions multiply.

The booth hasn't failed.

It has been reset to an earlier developmental stage—just at a larger, more expensive scale.

Why Growth Feels Like Betrayal

One of the most damaging emotional responses vendors experience is *confusion after improvement*.

They did the work.
They fixed the friction.
They stabilized the booth.

So when expansion makes things harder, it feels unfair.

This is where vendors begin questioning themselves:

"Maybe I misunderstood what was working."
"Maybe I overestimated demand."
"Maybe I'm not as good at this as I thought."

None of those conclusions are accurate.

The problem wasn't judgment.

It was timing.

Scaling Forces Compromises You Didn't Need to Make Yet

Early expansion introduces pressure that didn't exist before.

More space requires more inventory.
More inventory requires more cash.
More maintenance requires more time.
More decisions require more emotional energy.

Under that pressure, even disciplined vendors begin making concessions:

- Accepting slower turns "temporarily"
- Letting weaker items fill space
- Softening pricing discipline
- Explaining instead of clarifying

These aren't bad choices.

They're survival responses.

And once survival mode enters the system, trust and clarity begin eroding again—quietly, but consistently.

Why the Booth Feels Worse Even If Sales Improve

This is the part vendors struggle to articulate.

Sales may be higher.
Gross numbers may look better.

But the booth feels worse.

That's because effort increased faster than return.

When growth is earned, added effort is offset by increased clarity and confidence. When growth is premature, effort compounds without relief.

The booth starts demanding attention again.

And that demand is the signal something reset.

The Psychological Cost of Resetting the Clock

Resetting doesn't just affect performance.

It affects belief.

Vendors who experience one early expansion failure often hesitate the next time growth opportunities appear—even when they're truly ready. Momentum stalls not because the booth can't grow, but because trust in the process was damaged.

This is how vendors plateau *after* success.

Not because they failed.

Because they learned the wrong lesson from premature growth.

The Truth Most Vendors Miss

Scaling too early doesn't mean you can't scale.

It means you scaled **without reinforcement**.

Growth should make the booth easier to manage—not harder.

If expansion increases stress, confusion, or emotional load, the system wasn't ready to carry the weight.

That's not a moral failure.

It's a structural one.

This section is meant to feel uncomfortable.

It mirrors the lived experience of vendors who "did everything right" and still felt like they went backward.

That recognition is the warning.

Earned Expansion vs. Emotional Expansion

Most vendors don't scale because they're ready.

They scale because they're relieved.

Relief feels like momentum. It feels like permission. It feels like proof that the work finally paid off. After months—or years—of friction, hesitation, and uncertainty, the urge to *do more* is powerful.

But relief is not a growth signal.

It's an emotional one.

And confusing the two is how momentum breaks quietly.

Emotional Expansion: Growth Driven by Feeling

Emotional expansion happens when growth is driven by internal pressure instead of structural proof.

Sales stabilize, and the booth finally feels calm. The vendor starts thinking less about survival and more about possibility. That shift is natural—but dangerous if it isn't checked.

Emotional expansion often sounds reasonable:

"If this category works, I should double it."
"If this booth is steady, a bigger one would be smarter."
"If I don't act now, I'll lose momentum."

None of these thoughts are irrational.

They're just incomplete.

Emotional expansion tends to show up as:

- Adding categories before depth is proven

- Increasing inventory without understanding turn speed

- Expanding square footage to "keep up"

- Using growth as a way to relieve anxiety or boredom

The expansion itself isn't reckless.

The timing is.

Why Emotional Expansion Feels Justified

Emotional expansion is persuasive because it often follows success.

> Sales are better.
> Buyers respond positively.
> The booth feels validated.

So growth feels earned—even when it hasn't been reinforced.

This is where vendors confuse *improvement* with *durability*.

Improvement answers the question:
"Did something work?"

Durability answers a harder one:
"Will this still work when conditions change?"

Emotional expansion rarely waits for that answer.

Earned Expansion: Growth Driven by Proof

Earned expansion feels very different.

It's quiet.
Unrushed.
Almost anticlimactic.

Earned expansion happens after patterns repeat—not once, but consistently. It follows predictability, not excitement.

In earned expansion:

- Categories perform the same way month after month
- Restocking feels routine instead of urgent
- Slow periods don't trigger panic
- Decisions don't change under pressure

Expansion doesn't require new rules.

It extends existing ones.

That's the difference.

Reinforcement Comes Before Reach

Earned expansion reinforces what already works before extending it outward.

Before space increases:

- Depth is tested
- Standards are hardened
- Systems are stress-tested under normal fluctuations

Expansion isn't used to *find* success.

It's used to **scale known success** without changing behavior.

If growth requires new coping mechanisms, it isn't earned.

Why Earned Expansion Feels Unsatisfying

Earned expansion doesn't deliver a rush.

There's no dramatic pivot.
No sudden transformation.
No sense of "finally breaking free."

It often feels boring.

That boredom is the signal most vendors misinterpret.

> Boring growth is stable growth.
> Stable growth is survivable growth.

The booths that last aren't the ones that grew fastest.

They're the ones that grew without drama.

The Moment That Reveals Readiness

You're ready to expand when growth no longer feels like a solution.

When:

- Expansion doesn't relieve pressure
- Expansion doesn't fix a problem
- Expansion doesn't change behavior

It simply increases volume.

If growth feels like rescue, it's emotional.
If growth feels like reinforcement, it's earned.

The Final Contrast

Emotional expansion chases relief.
Earned expansion protects stability.

Emotional expansion creates motion.
Earned expansion preserves momentum.

Emotional expansion feels exciting.
Earned expansion feels obvious.

Only one of those survives long term.

Chapter Takeaway

Growth is not a reward for improvement.

It's a responsibility that exposes whether improvement was stable.

Scaling too early doesn't fail loudly.
It quietly dismantles what took months to build.

Earned expansion respects capacity.
It protects trust.
It preserves control.

When growth feels calm instead of urgent, you're ready.

And when you grow from that place, momentum doesn't break.

It multiplies.

The Cost of Standing Still

Most vendors don't quit because their booth fails.

They quit because it stalls.

Sales don't collapse. Rent still gets paid. A few items move each month. The booth looks "fine." From the outside, nothing appears broken enough to justify panic or drastic change. And that's exactly why the danger goes unnoticed.

Standing still feels responsible. It feels cautious. It feels like patience.

But in today's market, standing still is rarely neutral.

Markets don't pause. Customer expectations don't freeze. Shopping behavior doesn't wait for vendors to feel ready. While a booth maintains the same layout, the same inventory mix, the same pricing logic, the world around it keeps adjusting. What once felt stable quietly becomes outdated. What once sold reliably now needs help to move. What once felt like experience begins to look like rigidity.

The vendor doesn't feel like they're falling behind—until one day they realize they are.

This chapter exists because plateau is the most misunderstood phase of booth selling. Decline announces itself loudly: empty weeks, frustration, obvious loss. Plateau whispers. It disguises itself as "good enough." It convinces you that effort should ease because you've earned it. It rewards familiarity and punishes urgency.

And it costs more than most vendors realize.

The cost of standing still isn't always measured in lost dollars—at least not immediately.

It shows up first as hesitation.
Second-guessing.
Subtle resentment toward the market.

A growing sense that customers *"just don't buy like they used to,"* without a clear understanding of why. Inventory lingers longer. Restocks feel heavier instead of exciting. Booth work becomes maintenance instead of strategy.

Eventually, motivation erodes.

What makes this phase especially dangerous is that it often follows success.

Vendors who have already proven they can sell—who've survived early mistakes, learned their market, built a recognizable booth—are the most vulnerable to plateau.

They trust their instincts because those instincts once worked. They lean on patterns that used to be reliable. And slowly, without realizing it, they stop testing assumptions.

This chapter is not about fear-mongering. It's not a warning that every quiet month signals disaster.

It's about understanding that *inaction carries a cost*, even when things appear stable. Especially when they appear stable.

There's a difference between consistency and stagnation, and many vendors unknowingly cross that line.

Consistency is intentional. It's supported by observation, adjustment, and awareness.

Stagnation is passive. It assumes the booth will keep earning simply because it has in the past.

That assumption used to be safer than it is now.

The modern antique and vintage market is more crowded, more visual, and more choice-driven than it was even five years ago.

> Customers scroll faster.
> Compare more.
> Expect clarity.

They don't linger out of obligation. They respond to confidence, cohesion, and cues that signal relevance. When a booth doesn't evolve—even subtly—it fades into the background noise of the mall.

And fading doesn't feel dramatic. It feels quiet, gradual, and easy to explain away.

> *"I just need to give it more time."*
> *"It's probably seasonal."*
> *"The economy is weird right now."*

Those statements aren't always wrong—but they become dangerous when they replace analysis.

This chapter will challenge the idea that holding steady is inherently safe. It will examine how plateaus form, why experienced vendors miss the signs, and how comfort quietly undermines momentum.

We'll talk about the hidden costs—financial, emotional, and strategic—of staying in place too long.

Most importantly, this chapter will force a decision point.

Not a dramatic one. Not an all-or-nothing leap. But a clear recognition that every vendor eventually reaches a moment where standing still is no longer a neutral choice. Drift, reinvention, or exit—those are the paths, whether acknowledged or not.

You don't need to choose today.

But you do need to recognize where you are.

Because the market already has.

The Illusion of Stability

Stability is one of the most comforting lies a booth can tell you.

> It looks like rent paid on time.
> It looks like a handful of sales every week.
> It looks like customers stopping, browsing, occasionally buying.
> It looks like nothing's going wrong.

And that's the problem.

Most vendors define stability by absence of pain. If the booth isn't actively bleeding money, it must be fine. If sales haven't cratered, there's no urgency. If the booth still "works," then change can wait.

But stability, in practice, is not a fixed state. It's a relationship between your booth and the market—and the market is always moving. When the booth stays the same while customer behavior shifts, stability becomes an illusion created by lagging indicators.

> Rent is a lagging indicator.
> Sales totals are lagging indicators.
> Even foot traffic inside your booth is a lagging indicator.

They reflect what *has already happened*, not what's forming underneath the surface.

This is why many vendors are blindsided by decline. They don't feel it arriving. They don't see a cliff edge. They experience a long, flat stretch that feels calm—until they realize the ground has slowly tilted downward.

The illusion forms because early plateaus rarely remove revenue all at once. Instead, they stretch timelines. Items still sell, but slower. Profitable categories still work, but with less enthusiasm. Impulse buys become rarer. Customers browse more and commit less.

Nothing breaks. Everything just resists.

That resistance is often misread as external pressure: the economy, the season, changing tastes. Sometimes those factors are real—but stability becomes dangerous when vendors stop asking whether the booth itself is still aligned with how people shop *now*, not how they shopped when the booth peaked.

A stable booth can quietly lose relevance without losing visibility.

Customers still see it.
They just don't *feel* pulled toward it anymore.

This is where experienced vendors get trapped. Experience creates confidence. Confidence reduces urgency. And urgency is often what drives the small, necessary adjustments that keep a booth sharp. When things feel stable, those adjustments feel optional. Easy to postpone. Easy to rationalize away.

> *"I'll refresh after the holidays."*
> *"I'll deal with it next season."*
> *"It's not bad enough yet."*

But stability without evaluation is not safety—it's exposure.

The longer a booth sits unchanged, the more it relies on momentum created in the past. That momentum decays quietly. Layouts that once felt intuitive become invisible. Pricing that once felt competitive now feels vague. Inventory that once told a clear story starts to blur together.

The booth still exists. It just stops communicating clearly.

And customers respond to clarity.

They don't consciously think, *This booth hasn't evolved.*
They feel hesitation instead of excitement.
Uncertainty instead of confidence.
Disengagement instead of curiosity.

Those feelings don't show up on spreadsheets immediately.

They show up in behavior: fewer pickups, fewer walk-ins, fewer "I'll take this" moments. Vendors feel busier without feeling rewarded.

They spend more time rearranging instead of restocking. They touch the booth more but move it forward less.

This is the emotional tax of false stability.

> Work increases.
> Satisfaction decreases.
> Doubt creeps in—not sharply, but persistently.
> Vendors begin to question the market instead of the structure.

They assume demand disappeared rather than shifted.

What makes the illusion so powerful is that it doesn't feel like failure. It feels like maintenance. And maintenance feels responsible.

But maintenance alone does not sustain performance.

A booth that only maintains is borrowing relevance from its past. Eventually, the interest comes due.

True stability looks different than most vendors expect.

It doesn't feel static.
It feels responsive.
It includes small, ongoing corrections.
Minor layout refinements.
Inventory tweaks.
Pricing clarity.
Visual cues that signal intention instead of habit.

False stability resists those changes because nothing feels urgent enough to justify them.

That's why the illusion lasts so long.

By the time urgency finally appears, the booth is no longer standing still—it's already sliding. And recovery requires more effort than the earlier adjustments ever would have.

Recognizing this illusion isn't about creating anxiety. It's about restoring awareness. The goal is not to panic at every quiet week, but to stop using "fine" as a performance metric.

Fine is not a strategy. Fine is a pause button that only works on your side of the equation.

The market never pauses.

And the booths that survive long-term aren't the ones that never struggle—they're the ones that don't mistake stillness for safety.

Plateau vs. Decline (They Don't Look the Same at First)
Most vendors believe they'll recognize decline when it happens.

173

They expect it to announce itself loudly—empty weeks, alarming numbers, a sudden drop that demands action. Decline, in their mind, looks dramatic enough to force a response. Plateau, by contrast, feels harmless. Temporary. Manageable.

The problem is that plateau and decline don't begin as opposites. They begin as neighbors.

A plateau is not the absence of decline. It's the stage where decline hasn't become obvious yet.

This is why so many vendors misread what's happening in their booth. They sense that something has shifted, but because sales haven't collapsed, they assume the booth is holding steady. In reality, the booth has stopped advancing while the market continues moving forward.

The earliest difference between plateau and decline is not revenue—it's friction.

Plateau introduces resistance. Decline removes motion altogether.

In a plateau, items still sell, but they take longer. Customers still browse, but fewer commit. You still restock, but the restocks don't create the same lift they used to. The booth works harder to produce the same results.

Decline comes later, when that resistance turns into silence.

But most vendors wait for silence before they act.

The warning signs of plateau are subtle and easy to rationalize away.

Inventory lingers just long enough to feel annoying, but not long enough to trigger alarm.

You notice yourself explaining slow movement more often—seasonality, foot traffic, the economy—without adjusting the booth itself.

You feel busy, but not effective.

These are not neutral signals. They're early indicators that alignment is slipping.

One of the clearest distinctions between plateau and decline is how effort behaves.

In a healthy booth, effort compounds. Small actions create visible results. A tweak to layout improves flow. A new category sparks interest. A restock creates momentum.

In a plateau, effort dissipates.

You do the work, but the response is muted. Rearrangements feel cosmetic. New items blend in instead of standing out. Pricing changes don't move the needle the way they once did. The booth absorbs effort without reflecting it back.

That's not laziness. It's misalignment.

Decline, on the other hand, feels empty. Effort stops because motivation collapses. Plateau is more dangerous because effort continues—but without payoff. Vendors burn energy trying to revive results using tools that no longer fit the problem.

Another difference lies in customer behavior.

During plateau, customers don't avoid the booth.

> They hesitate.
> They pause longer.
> They pick items up and put them back more often. They browse without urgency.

The booth remains visible, but it no longer creates clear desire.

This is often mistaken for "customers just browsing these days," but browsing without buying is not random. It's feedback. It signals uncertainty, not disinterest.

Decline happens when that uncertainty turns into indifference.

The reason plateau is so easy to miss is because it doesn't feel like loss—it feels like waiting.

Vendors tell themselves they're between cycles. Between seasons. Between trends. Between good months.

Waiting feels reasonable. It feels patient. But waiting without diagnosis is not patience—it's avoidance.

Another critical distinction is emotional response. Decline produces panic. Plateau produces irritation.

Vendors in decline are scared. Vendors in plateau are frustrated.

Frustration is easier to live with. It doesn't force big decisions. It invites small complaints instead. About pricing pressure. About customers. About online competition. About the mall itself.

And while those complaints may contain truth, they often distract from the real issue: the booth is no longer clearly signaling why it deserves attention *now*.

Plateau also tricks vendors into thinking they've already done the hard part.

> They've survived early mistakes.
> They've figured out their niche.
> They've learned what sells.

So when performance flattens, they assume endurance is the answer rather than evolution.

But endurance only works when conditions remain stable—and they never do.

Decline is what happens when plateau goes unaddressed long enough that the booth loses its voice entirely. By then, recovery is harder.

> More changes are required.
> More emotional energy is needed.
> Confidence is lower. Doubt is louder.

That's why the smartest intervention point is here—when the booth still functions, but not freely.

Recognizing plateau requires a shift in how success is measured. Not just by whether sales happen, but by how easily they happen. Not by whether effort exists, but by whether effort converts.

If the booth demands more attention to produce the same outcome, something is wrong—even if the numbers don't yet look alarming.

Plateau is the market asking a question.

Decline is the market answering it for you.

The earlier you listen, the more control you keep.

When Experience Becomes a Liability

Experience is one of the most valuable assets a vendor can have—until it quietly stops being questioned.

Early on, experience is earned the hard way. Through mistakes, slow months, overbuying, underpricing, poor layouts, and trial-and-error learning.

Every lesson improves judgment. Patterns emerge. Instincts sharpen. Confidence grows for good reason.

The danger begins when those instincts stop being tested.

What once functioned as adaptive knowledge gradually hardens into assumption.

> *"This is what sells here."*
> *"This price point works."*
> *"Customers around here don't buy that."*

Each statement may have been true at one time, but time erodes accuracy faster than most vendors realize.

The market does not reward experience—it rewards relevance.

Experienced vendors often miss this shift because experience *feels* like mastery.

> Mastery implies stability.
> Stability implies fewer changes are needed.

And that belief subtly lowers curiosity.

>Fewer experiments.
>Fewer risks.
>Fewer questions.

The booth becomes efficient—but not responsive.

One of the most common liabilities of experience is pattern over-reliance.

Vendors learn what worked and then unconsciously build guardrails around it. They stop exploring outside those boundaries because past success reinforces the belief that the formula is complete.

But formulas expire.

Trends don't need to change dramatically to invalidate a pattern. Sometimes all that shifts is customer expectation: cleaner presentation, clearer pricing, faster visual payoff. When those expectations rise, older methods don't fail—they just underperform.

Underperformance is easy to ignore when sales still happen.

Experience also creates blind spots around layout and flow. A vendor who has worked their booth for years no longer sees it the way customers do.

>They know where everything is.
>They understand the logic behind placement.
>They recognize categories instantly.

Customers don't have that context.

What feels obvious to the vendor may feel cluttered, ambiguous, or overwhelming to a shopper. Experience can make vendors forget how first impressions work because they stopped experiencing them firsthand.

Another subtle liability is emotional investment. The longer a vendor has been in the booth, the more history is attached to certain items, categories, or display choices.

"That line always sold well for me."
"That piece style built my booth."
"Customers always commented on this section."

History creates loyalty—but not all loyalty serves the future.

When emotional attachment replaces performance evaluation, change feels personal. Removing an underperforming category feels like erasing part of your identity rather than making a strategic decision. That emotional friction slows necessary action.

Experienced vendors also tend to overvalue durability of demand. They assume certain items will always sell because they always have. But demand is not static—it's situational. It depends on context, presentation, alternatives, and shopper mood.

An item that sold effortlessly three years ago may now require explanation, repositioning, or retirement. Experience often delays that realization because memory overrides observation.

There's also a confidence trap around pricing. Vendors who have priced successfully in the past trust their numbers. They assume resistance is temporary rather than structural. They hesitate to simplify or clarify pricing because they believe customers "should understand" the value.

But modern shoppers don't reward explanations—they reward immediacy.

If value isn't obvious quickly, attention moves on.

Experience can also dull urgency.

New vendors watch every sale closely. They notice shifts immediately because everything is fragile.

Experienced vendors, by contrast, expect variance. They tolerate slowness longer. They give the booth more time to "work itself out."

That patience can be wise—but it can also delay intervention until momentum is already lost.

The irony is that experienced vendors have the best tools to adapt.

> They know how to source.
> They know their margins.
> They understand operations.

But those tools are only effective when paired with willingness to question assumptions.

Experience becomes an asset again the moment it regains flexibility.

The vendors who thrive long-term are not the ones with the most years behind them—they're the ones who remain observant despite those years. They treat experience as a reference point, not a rulebook. They test small changes. They watch customer behavior more than their own preferences.

They allow experience to inform decisions, not dictate them.

This section isn't about discarding what you've learned. It's about recognizing when learning has stopped. Experience should shorten the feedback loop—not close it.

If your booth relies on past success to justify present performance, experience has become a liability.

In the next section, we'll look at what that liability actually costs—because the damage isn't limited to sales numbers. It spreads into energy, capital, and motivation in ways most vendors underestimate.

The Hidden Costs of Inaction

Inaction feels harmless because it doesn't look like a decision.

There's no moment where you sign off on decline. No line you cross that says, *I've chosen to stop improving this booth.*

Instead, inaction disguises itself as patience, caution, or realism. You tell yourself you're waiting for the right moment, the right season, the right signal.

But while inaction feels passive, its costs accumulate aggressively.

The most obvious cost is financial—but it's also the least understood.

When a booth plateaus, it doesn't just lose money it *should* be making. It ties up capital that could be working elsewhere.

Inventory that lingers longer than necessary locks cash into items that no longer earn efficiently. That money can't be reinvested into faster-moving categories, better presentation tools, or smarter experiments.

Over time, that trapped capital compounds the problem. The booth becomes less flexible precisely when flexibility is most needed.

But the financial cost goes deeper than inventory drag.

Opportunity cost is invisible, which makes it easy to ignore. Vendors often calculate success by asking, *Did I make money?* instead of *Did I maximize what this space could have earned?*

A plateau booth may still be profitable—but it's quietly underperforming its potential. That gap widens over time. And once you realize it exists, catching up requires far more effort than incremental adjustments would have.

Then there's the emotional cost.

Inaction drains motivation in a way failure does not. Failure creates urgency. It demands problem-solving. Inaction creates frustration without resolution. Vendors feel stuck—working, adjusting, rearranging—but not progressing.

That emotional friction builds slowly. The booth stops feeling rewarding. Restocks feel heavy. Booth visits feel like chores instead of opportunities. You start to resent the time it demands because the return feels muted.

Eventually, that resentment bleeds outward.

Toward customers.

> Toward the market.
> Toward the mall.
> Toward online competition.

The booth becomes a source of tension rather than pride.

This emotional cost is one of the leading reasons vendors burn out—even when their booths are still technically "successful."

Inaction also creates cognitive debt.

Every week you avoid making a decision, the mental load grows. You know something needs attention, but you haven't clarified what or why.

That unresolved tension takes up mental bandwidth. You think about the booth more, but with less clarity. You replay questions instead of answering them.

> Should I change this section?
> Should I try something new?
> Is it even worth it anymore?

Unanswered questions drain energy faster than hard answers.

There's also a strategic cost that's easy to miss: lost learning.

When you don't test changes, you don't gather feedback. When you don't gather feedback, you don't refine strategy. Inaction freezes your understanding of the market at an outdated point in time.

You assume you know what customers want—but you're no longer verifying it.

This is dangerous because confidence without data feels the same as confidence with it.

Vendors believe they're informed when they're actually relying on memory. That makes eventual adjustments feel riskier than they are, because uncertainty has grown unchecked.

Inaction doesn't preserve certainty—it increases it.

Another hidden cost is erosion of momentum.

Momentum isn't just about sales volume. It's about responsiveness.

A booth with momentum reacts quickly. Small changes produce noticeable shifts. Feedback loops are tight. Adjustments feel worthwhile.

In a plateau, momentum decays. Changes feel heavier. Results take longer. Effort-to-reward ratios worsen. Vendors interpret this as proof that change "doesn't work anymore," when in reality the delay is the result of too much time spent standing still.

Momentum, once lost, is harder to rebuild than it is to maintain.

Finally, inaction costs agency.

The longer you wait, the fewer choices feel available. Inventory ages. Confidence erodes. The idea of reinvention feels daunting instead of manageable. Vendors begin to frame decisions in terms of escape rather than growth.

> *"Maybe I should downsize."*
> *"Maybe I should take a break."*
> *"Maybe this just isn't worth it anymore."*

Those thoughts don't appear because the market is impossible. They appear because agency has slowly been surrendered through delay.

Action preserves options. Inaction narrows them.

The irony is that most of the changes that prevent these costs are small. Clarifying pricing. Tightening layout. Testing a new category. Removing underperformers. These are not dramatic pivots—but they require willingness to act *before* pain demands it.

Standing still doesn't keep the booth safe.

It quietly increases the cost of every future decision.

And the longer you wait, the higher that cost becomes.

Comfort Is the Enemy of Momentum

Comfort is often mistaken for confidence.

A comfortable booth feels familiar. You know where everything is. You know what usually sells. You understand your routines—when to restock, how often to rearrange, which categories deserve attention. There's a rhythm to it, and rhythm feels like control.

But comfort is not momentum.

Momentum creates movement. Comfort preserves position.

The problem is that comfort doesn't announce itself as danger. It presents as efficiency. It tells you that you've earned ease—that after years of effort, the booth should finally feel manageable. And to some extent, that's true. Systems should simplify work over time.

But when ease replaces intention, momentum stalls.

Comfort encourages repetition.

> **You restock the same** types of items because sourcing them is easier.
> **You keep the same layout** because it works well enough.
> **You price within familiar ranges** because they feel safe.

None of these choices are wrong on their own—but together, they create sameness.

Sameness is invisible to returning customers.

Regular shoppers stop seeing what hasn't changed. Even new customers subconsciously register when a booth lacks contrast or surprise.

> Without novelty, urgency disappears.
> Browsing becomes casual.
> Decisions slow down.

Comfort also dulls risk tolerance. When a booth is stable, experimentation feels unnecessary. Why gamble when things are fine? But that mindset assumes that risk only comes from change—not from stagnation.

In reality, refusing to test is its own risk.

Momentum thrives on small, intentional disruptions. A new focal point. A refined category. A clearer price signal. These aren't reckless moves, they're feedback mechanisms. They create contrast, and contrast creates attention.

Comfort smooths out those disruptions. It prioritizes predictability over discovery. Over time, the booth stops surprising customers—and eventually stops surprising you.

Another way comfort undermines momentum is through routine-driven work. Vendors in comfort mode stay busy, but the work is repetitive.

> Straightening.
> Minor rearranging.
> Dusting.
> Touching items without altering meaning.

The booth receives attention—but not direction.

Work without direction feels productive in the moment, but it doesn't move the booth forward. When results don't improve, vendors assume they need to work harder, not differently. That's when burnout begins to creep in.

Comfort also affects decision speed. In a booth with momentum, decisions are quick because feedback is clear.

> You know what's working.
> You know what isn't.
> You adjust accordingly.

In a comfortable but stagnant booth, decisions drag.

You hesitate to remove items because they might sell.
You delay changes because they don't feel urgent.
You rationalize holding patterns because they're familiar.

Delayed decisions accumulate. And each delay reinforces the illusion that waiting is safer than acting.

The most dangerous aspect of comfort is that it disguises itself as earned wisdom. Vendors believe they've "seen enough" to trust their instincts implicitly. But instincts require calibration. Without new data, they drift out of alignment.

Comfort slowly replaces curiosity.

You stop asking why something sold—or didn't.
You stop noticing subtle shifts in customer behavior.
You stop questioning assumptions because the booth feels predictable.

But predictability is only valuable when demand remains constant. When demand shifts, predictability becomes a liability.

Momentum doesn't require constant upheaval. It requires responsiveness. The willingness to notice friction and address it early. The courage to disrupt comfort before discomfort forces you to.

The booths that maintain momentum over years are not chaotic— they're intentional. They create controlled discomfort through regular evaluation. They test small changes before the market demands big ones.

Comfort feels like rest. Momentum feels like engagement.

One preserves energy in the short term. The other preserves relevance over time.

If your booth feels easy but not exciting—familiar but not rewarding, it may not be stable. It may simply be comfortable.

And comfort, left unchecked, quietly drains momentum until restarting it feels overwhelming.

In the next section, we'll look at the moment every vendor eventually reaches—the point where comfort, stagnation, and frustration converge into a decision whether acknowledged or not.

The Vendor Decision Point

Every vendor reaches a moment where standing still is no longer passive.

It doesn't arrive with a deadline or a clear announcement. There's no single bad week that forces it. Instead, it forms gradually as plateau, comfort, and frustration overlap. At some point, the booth stops feeling like it's moving forward—and the vendor senses that something has to change.

This is the decision point.

Most vendors don't recognize it when they're in it. They feel unsettled, restless, dissatisfied—but they don't label those feelings as a crossroads.

They assume they're just tired.
Or discouraged.
Or dealing with a rough stretch.

But beneath those emotions is a structural reality: the booth can't remain as it is without consequences.

At this point, every vendor has three paths available—whether they consciously choose one or not.

The first path is drift.

Drift is what happens when no decision is made. The booth remains mostly unchanged. Minor adjustments occur, but nothing fundamental shifts.

> Inventory ages.
> Momentum fades further.
> Effort continues, but with diminishing returns.

Drift feels safe because it avoids risk. But drift is not neutral. It slowly transfers control to the market.

Outcomes become reactive instead of intentional. Vendors stop steering and start enduring.

The second path is reinvention.

Reinvention doesn't mean starting over. It means re-engaging strategically. Evaluating alignment. Questioning assumptions. Making targeted changes based on observation rather than habit.

This path requires effort—but it preserves agency. Vendors regain clarity. Decisions become purposeful again. Momentum begins to rebuild because the booth responds to intervention.

Reinvention is uncomfortable, but it's controlled discomfort. The kind that restores confidence rather than erodes it.

The third path is exit.

Exit doesn't always mean quitting immediately. Sometimes it looks like downsizing. Reducing effort. Letting the booth run on autopilot until the lease ends. Emotionally checking out before physically leaving.

Exit can be the right choice for some vendors. But it's rarely chosen cleanly. More often, it's the result of prolonged drift and frustration. By the time vendors consider leaving, confidence is low and options feel limited.

What matters most is not which path you choose—it's whether you choose deliberately.

Drift is what happens when choice is avoided.

This decision point is uncomfortable because it forces honesty. It asks whether the booth still aligns with your goals, your energy, and your expectations. It challenges the belief that time alone will fix misalignment.

Many vendors hope for a signal big enough to justify action. A bad month. A policy change. A rent increase. Something external that makes the decision feel necessary.

But waiting for permission from the market is another form of surrender.

The market doesn't give permission—it gives feedback.

And at this stage, the feedback is subtle but clear: what worked before is no longer sufficient.

Reinvention doesn't require dramatic overhaul. It requires engagement. The willingness to step back, assess, and act before frustration turns into resignation.

This chapter isn't pushing you toward reinvention yet—that comes next. But it's important to recognize that indecision itself is a path, and it rarely leads anywhere you'd choose intentionally.

The decision point is where ownership returns to the vendor.

You either let the booth slowly decide for you, or you step back into control.

There is no moral judgment here. Drift, reinvention, and exit are all outcomes vendors experience. The difference between regret and clarity often lies in whether the decision was conscious.

In the final section, we'll reframe what growth actually means—because many vendors avoid reinvention not because they don't want progress, but because they misunderstand what growth demands.

Reframing Growth Before We Talk Tactics

For many vendors, the word *growth* triggers resistance before it triggers curiosity.

> Growth sounds expensive.
> It sounds exhausting.
> It sounds like bigger booths, more inventory, higher risk, and less margin for error.

So when the idea of reinvention appears, it's often dismissed—not because vendors don't want improvement, but because they assume improvement demands expansion.

That assumption is wrong.

Growth is not about scale. It's about alignment.

Most plateaued booths aren't failing because they're too small. They're failing because the signals they send no longer match how customers decide. Growth, in this context, means restoring clarity—not adding weight.

This is why so many vendors avoid change longer than they should. They imagine growth as a commitment to *more* when what's actually required is *better*. Better communication. Better flow. Better intent.

Reframing growth starts by stripping away the myths attached to it.

Growth does not mean more inventory.
In many cases, it means less—fewer categories, tighter selection, clearer purpose.

Growth does not mean higher prices.
It often means clearer pricing—less friction, fewer questions, faster decisions.

Growth does not mean bigger risk.
It means smaller, more frequent tests that reduce uncertainty over time.

When vendors equate growth with expansion, they trap themselves in inaction. Expansion feels like a leap. Alignment feels like a step.

And steps are manageable.

True growth restores responsiveness. It shortens the distance between action and feedback. When alignment improves, effort converts again. Changes matter. Adjustments register. Momentum returns not because you're doing more—but because what you're doing finally matches what the market is responding to *now*.

This is why growth often feels quieter than expected.

There's no dramatic transformation. No overnight surge. Instead, there's a reduction in resistance. Items move with less explanation. Layouts feel easier to navigate. Customers commit faster. Booth visits feel purposeful again.

Growth feels like relief before it feels like excitement.

Another misconception is that growth requires abandoning what made the booth successful. In reality, it requires understanding *why* those things worked—and whether they still do. Some elements will remain. Others will need refinement or removal.

Reinvention is not rejection of the past. It's translation.

The vendors who struggle most at this stage are those who treat growth as an identity threat. They fear that changing the booth means admitting past decisions were wrong. But evolution doesn't invalidate earlier success—it builds on it.

Markets shift. Context changes. Adaptation is not an apology.

Reframing growth also means redefining success metrics. Growth isn't just higher sales totals. It's improved efficiency. Faster sell-through. Lower emotional friction. Clearer decision-making.

A booth that earns the same revenue with less stress has grown—even if the numbers look unchanged.

And a booth that earns slightly more with significantly more resistance has not.

Before tactics matter, mindset must adjust. If growth is framed as pressure, vendors resist it. If growth is framed as alignment, vendors engage.

That's why this chapter stops here.

Before discussing *how* to move forward, it's necessary to clarify *what moving forward actually means*. Without that clarity, tactics feel overwhelming. With it, they feel logical.

Standing still is not safe—but movement doesn't have to be reckless.

In the next chapter, we'll begin translating awareness into action. Not with sweeping changes, but with deliberate recalibration. We'll focus on identifying where alignment has slipped—and how to restore it without burning energy or confidence.

Because growth isn't about chasing momentum.

It's about removing what's been quietly blocking it.

Chapter Takeaway

Standing still doesn't announce itself as a mistake.

It feels reasonable. Measured. Responsible. Especially for vendors who have already proven they can sell. But over time, stillness extracts a cost—first in momentum, then in clarity, and eventually in control.

This chapter wasn't about diagnosing failure. It was about recognizing a phase many successful vendors pass through without naming. Plateau is not the opposite of growth—it's what happens when growth is deferred too long.

The good news is that this phase is reversible.

Nothing in this chapter suggests you're behind beyond repair. In fact, recognizing these patterns early is what preserves options. Awareness restores agency. And agency is what allows intentional movement rather than reactive change.

> You don't need urgency driven by fear.
> You need direction driven by clarity.

In the chapters ahead, we'll move out of diagnosis and into recalibration—how to re-engage the booth strategically, restore responsiveness, and rebuild momentum without expanding stress.

Not by doing more.
By doing what matters again.

The Vendor Plateau and Why Most Never Break It

When Nothing Is Technically Wrong

There is a phase of booth ownership that feels deceptively safe.

Sales are still happening. Rent gets paid. You aren't panicking when the end of the month approaches. Inventory moves—slowly, predictably, just enough to keep the lights on. Nothing is on fire. Nothing is collapsing. From the outside, the booth looks healthy enough.

And that's exactly why this phase is so dangerous.

Most vendors don't fail because their booth stops working. They fail because it works *just enough* to remove urgency—but not enough to create progress. The booth enters a holding pattern. Months start to blur together. The numbers don't crash, but they don't climb either. And because there's no obvious problem to fix, nothing meaningful changes.

This is the vendor plateau.

It doesn't announce itself with warning signs. There's no dramatic drop in sales, no clear reason to panic, no single bad decision to point to. Instead, it arrives quietly, disguised as stability. You tell yourself you're "doing fine." You remind yourself that the market is tough. You say things like, "At least it's steady," or "This is just how it is right now."

And technically, you're not wrong.

But technically right is how vendors get stuck for years.

The plateau phase is where effort and outcome stop matching. You still restock. You still clean. You still tweak displays and adjust prices and post on social media when you can. You are *working*. Yet the booth refuses to respond the way it once did. The early growth you remember—the excitement, the momentum, the feeling that each improvement mattered—has vanished.

193

What replaces it is maintenance.

Maintenance feels productive, but it's not growth. It keeps the booth alive, not advancing. And because maintenance tasks are familiar and emotionally comfortable, they slowly become the entirety of the business. The booth becomes something you manage instead of something you build.

This is where many vendors unknowingly spend the majority of their booth careers.

They don't quit. They don't fail out. They simply stall.

The problem is that plateaus don't create pain strong enough to force change. There's no crisis to react to. No emergency meeting with yourself. No moment where the answer feels obvious. Instead, there's a low-grade frustration that never quite boils over—just enough dissatisfaction to feel tired, but not enough to feel bold.

Over time, that quiet tension turns inward.

You start questioning the market instead of the structure of your booth. You blame foot traffic, the economy, social media algorithms, or "the type of customers we get now." You watch newer vendors surge past you and explain it away as luck, novelty, or underpricing. You tell yourself your booth is "more curated," "more niche," or "more consistent."

All of those explanations feel reasonable. None of them solve the problem.

The truth is this: plateaus are not caused by laziness, lack of passion, or bad work ethic. In fact, many of the vendors most stuck in a plateau are the ones working the hardest. They care deeply. They're invested emotionally. They've built an identity around their booth.

That attachment is part of what keeps them frozen.

Because breaking a plateau requires questioning things that feel settled—inventory choices you've defended for years, layouts you've grown comfortable with, pricing strategies you've normalized, and assumptions you no longer remember forming. It requires acknowledging that what *worked* may now be what's *limiting* you.

And that's uncomfortable.

So instead, most vendors adjust around the plateau rather than through it. They learn to live inside the ceiling rather than challenge it. They settle into routines that feel responsible and safe. They accept stability as success.

This chapter is not here to shame that choice.

It's here to name it.

Because once you can recognize a plateau for what it is—not a failure, not a judgment, not a verdict—you can finally decide whether you're willing to stay inside it... or ready to move beyond it.

The Illusion of "Doing Fine"

"Doing fine" is one of the most dangerous phrases in booth selling.

It sounds reasonable. Responsible, even. It signals that you're not panicking, not reckless, not making emotional decisions. In a business where volatility is common, "fine" feels like a win. And on paper, it often is—sales are covering rent, inventory isn't piling up uncontrollably, and nothing is screaming for immediate attention.

But "fine" is not a neutral state. It's a decision point disguised as stability.

When a booth is truly failing, action is obvious. You either fix what's broken or you exit. There's clarity in that kind of pressure. When a booth is growing, momentum pulls you forward. Improvements feel rewarded. Risk feels justified. Growth creates its own energy.

The plateau sits between those two extremes—and that's where "fine" becomes a trap.

Vendors in this phase aren't ignoring their booths. They're maintaining them. They restock when something sells. They straighten displays. They adjust pricing on pieces that linger too long. They show up consistently and do what they believe responsible vendors are supposed to do. From the outside, there's no clear reason to intervene.

And because nothing is obviously wrong, nothing is questioned deeply.

This is where stagnation becomes socially acceptable.

Antique malls unintentionally reinforce this mindset. When a vendor pays rent on time, keeps their space tidy, and doesn't complain, they're viewed as a "good vendor." Performance rarely enters the conversation unless it becomes a problem. Quiet consistency is rewarded with silence. No one pulls you aside and says, "You're stuck." No one challenges your numbers as long as they're not declining.

So "fine" becomes normalized.

Over time, vendors start using external explanations to justify the lack of growth. The market is slow. Customers are more cautious. Everyone is struggling right now. These statements may contain truth, but they also provide cover. They shift responsibility away from structure and toward circumstances—things that feel out of your control.

That shift matters.

Because once growth stalls, the most important question isn't *why sales aren't higher*. It's *why nothing you do seems to move the needle anymore*. Vendors stuck in "fine" mode often feel like they're doing all the right things, yet results remain stubbornly unchanged. The booth becomes resistant to effort.

That resistance is easy to misinterpret.

Instead of recognizing a ceiling, vendors assume they need to try harder. They add more inventory. They run small sales. They rearrange without intention. They post more frequently online. Each action feels productive, but none of it creates meaningful lift. The booth absorbs effort without responding.

That's when frustration sets in.

But frustration doesn't always lead to insight. More often, it leads to resignation. Vendors lower expectations quietly. They stop setting sales goals. They measure success by survival instead of progress. They tell themselves the booth is "just extra income now" or "more of a hobby than a business," even though they still rely on the money.

"Doing fine" becomes a way to protect yourself from disappointment.

The danger is that this mindset slowly rewrites your relationship with the booth. You stop asking what it *could* be and focus only on keeping it where it is. Risk begins to feel irresponsible rather than necessary. Change starts to feel like disruption instead of opportunity.

And because nothing breaks, nothing forces the issue.

Years can pass in this state. Vendors wake up one day realizing they've been working the same booth, the same way, for far longer than they intended—without the growth they once imagined. The booth didn't fail them. It simply never evolved.

The truth is uncomfortable but important: most plateaus aren't caused by bad luck or bad markets. They're caused by unchallenged assumptions. "Fine" becomes the ceiling because it's never interrogated.

Recognizing that illusion is the first real step forward.

Once you admit that "doing fine" isn't enough—not because it's wrong, but because it's limiting—you create space for better questions. And better questions are what break plateaus.

The Invisible Ceiling Every Booth Hits

Every booth has a ceiling.

Not a motivational ceiling. Not a mindset ceiling. A structural one.

This is the part most vendors resist, because it challenges a deeply held belief: that more effort should always produce more results. In the early stages of booth selling, that belief feels true. You add inventory, sales increase. You improve your display, pieces move faster. You price more intentionally, margins improve. The relationship between work and outcome feels direct and reliable.

Then, without warning, it stops.

The booth reaches a point where added effort no longer produces meaningful gains. Sales level off. Monthly numbers fluctuate within a narrow band. Good months are followed by average ones. Average months look exactly like the months before them. You're busy—but you're not advancing.

That's the ceiling.

What makes this ceiling so hard to see is that it isn't caused by one obvious limitation. It's created by the combined effect of decisions that once worked perfectly. Inventory type. Price range. Display density. Customer expectations. Even the physical footprint of the booth itself. Together, these elements define how much revenue your space can reasonably produce in its current form.

Once that ceiling is reached, the booth stops responding to incremental change.

Adding more inventory doesn't raise the ceiling—it just increases crowding. Running small discounts doesn't raise the ceiling—it compresses margins. Rearranging displays without changing intent doesn't raise the ceiling—it just shifts the same pieces around the same space.

From the vendor's perspective, it feels unfair.

You're doing more than you used to. You're paying closer attention. You're trying to be proactive. Yet the booth seems indifferent. That indifference often gets misread as market fatigue or customer disinterest, but the reality is simpler and more frustrating: the booth has taught you everything it can in its current configuration.

This is where many vendors make the wrong adjustment.

Instead of recognizing the ceiling, they attempt to push against it harder. They bring in more product to "give customers more options." They widen their inventory mix, hoping variety will unlock sales. They lower prices slightly to encourage movement. All of these changes feel logical—and all of them stay safely within the same structure.

The ceiling remains untouched.

The core issue is that ceilings are not broken by volume. They're broken by redesign.

But redesign requires acknowledging that the booth, as it exists, is optimized for its current results—not future ones. That can feel like a personal indictment. After all, this booth reflects your taste, your eye, your time, and often your identity. Admitting it has limits can feel like admitting *you* have limits.

You don't.
Your structure does.

Every antique mall has booths that illustrate this perfectly. Vendors who work constantly yet never break past the same monthly average. Vendors who restock weekly but sell the same dollar amount month after month. Vendors who feel exhausted not because they're failing—but because they're pushing against a wall they can't see.

What makes this ceiling invisible is that nothing collapses when you hit it. The booth doesn't stop selling. It doesn't demand attention. It simply refuses to grow.

And because the booth still "works," vendors assume the solution must be incremental: a little more inventory, a little more effort, a little more time. The idea that the entire configuration might need to change feels extreme—especially when nothing is technically broken.

But this is where growth stalls permanently for many vendors.

Effort and outcome become disconnected. You stop trusting feedback because the booth no longer responds clearly. Improvements feel arbitrary. Success feels random. And when results don't change, motivation erodes—not because you don't care, but because you don't know what lever to pull anymore.

That confusion is the hallmark of a ceiling.

The important realization here is this: ceilings are not punishments. They're signals. They exist because a structure has matured. The booth has stabilized. It has found equilibrium. That equilibrium can support consistent income—but it cannot support expansion without intentional disruption.

Once you understand that, the plateau stops feeling like a personal failure and starts looking like a design problem.

And design problems, unlike motivational ones, can actually be solved.

Busy Isn't Momentum

One of the most misleading aspects of the vendor plateau is how productive it feels.

You are doing things. Constantly. There is always something to clean, restock, straighten, price, tag, or rearrange. The booth demands attention, and you respond. On the surface, this looks like momentum. Activity creates the illusion of progress, especially when effort has historically led to results.

But activity is not the same as movement.

Momentum has direction. Busy just has motion.

This distinction matters because most vendors stuck at a plateau aren't idle—they're exhausted. They're spending time in the booth, thinking about the booth, sourcing for the booth, and worrying about the booth. The problem isn't a lack of engagement. It's that the engagement is no longer strategic.

Restocking is a perfect example.

In a growth phase, restocking expands capacity. You replace sold items with better ones. You test new categories. You refine what works and remove what doesn't. Each restock is an opportunity to learn and adjust.

In a plateau, restocking becomes maintenance. You replace sold items with similar ones. You refill gaps without questioning why they exist. The booth stays full, but nothing changes. Inventory cycles, but the structure remains frozen.

The same thing happens with cleaning and organizing.

Straightening shelves, dusting displays, and making the booth look "nice" are necessary—but they don't create momentum on their own. When a booth is stuck, these tasks often become a substitute for harder decisions. They feel productive without requiring risk. They improve appearance without challenging performance.

Even rearranging can fall into this trap.

Many vendors rearrange their booth frequently while leaving its underlying logic untouched. The same types of items stay grouped together. The same price bands dominate the space. The same visual rhythm repeats itself. Customers may see something slightly different, but their buying behavior doesn't change because their experience hasn't fundamentally shifted.

Online activity can create the same illusion.

Posting on social media feels like progress. Sharing new finds, staging photos, and engaging with followers gives the sense that you're "doing something to grow." But if the booth itself hasn't changed structurally, online visibility often just feeds the same ceiling. Attention comes in, behavior stays the same.

This is why plateaued vendors often feel confused.

They're not lazy. They're not disengaged. They're doing all the things they're "supposed" to do—yet nothing improves. Over time, that disconnect erodes confidence. You start wondering if effort even matters anymore.

It does—but only when it's aligned with change.

Momentum isn't created by doing more of what you already do. It's created by shifting what the booth *is*. That's uncomfortable because it requires stepping out of routines that feel safe and familiar. Busy work is predictable. Strategic change is uncertain.

So vendors choose busy.

They mistake motion for movement. They confuse upkeep with advancement. They exhaust themselves maintaining a structure that has already reached its limit.

The hardest part is that busyness can delay realization indefinitely. As long as you're occupied, you don't have to confront the plateau directly. You can tell yourself you're "working on it." You can feel responsible without feeling exposed.

But eventually, fatigue replaces hope.

The booth doesn't feel exciting anymore. It feels heavy. The joy that once came from sourcing and setting up is replaced by obligation. At that point, many vendors assume they're burned out—when in reality, they're just stuck.

Understanding this difference is critical.

Because once you stop equating activity with progress, you can finally evaluate whether your effort is moving the booth forward—or simply keeping it in place.

Comfort Is the Real Risk

The most powerful force holding vendors in a plateau isn't fear of failure.

It's comfort.

Not the obvious kind. Not laziness or indifference. This is earned comfort—the kind that comes from experience, familiarity, and having survived the early chaos of booth selling. You know what sells *enough*. You know how to source reliably. You know how to keep the booth presentable and profitable within a narrow range.

That knowledge creates confidence.

And that confidence quietly hardens into constraint.

Over time, vendors begin to protect what feels stable. Inventory choices become safer. Pricing becomes predictable. Layouts stop evolving and start repeating. Not because the vendor lacks ideas, but because they've learned which risks *aren't necessary* to maintain income. The booth stops being a place of experimentation and becomes a place of preservation.

This is where comfort becomes dangerous.

Because growth doesn't happen inside what already works—it happens when something that works is deliberately disrupted. That disruption feels irresponsible when stability has been hard-earned. Vendors who have paid their dues don't want to gamble with what they've built. They've invested time, money, and identity into the booth, and risking that feels personal.

So instead, they optimize for peace.

They avoid big changes. They defend long-standing categories even when margins flatten. They keep pieces that "should sell eventually" because letting them go feels wasteful. They explain stagnation as intentional curation rather than structural inertia.

Identity plays a major role here.

Many booths become extensions of the vendor's taste and personality. "This is my style" becomes a justification for consistency—even when consistency has turned into rigidity. Feedback that challenges the booth can feel like feedback about the person. Suggestions are interpreted as criticism rather than opportunity.

This emotional entanglement makes plateaus stickier.

New vendors, ironically, are often more flexible. They're still learning. They're still testing. They haven't yet attached their sense of self to their booth's layout or inventory mix. Long-term vendors, on the other hand, have history. And history creates attachment.

Attachment creates resistance.

The irony is that comfort often feels like success. You're no longer scrambling. You're not stressed every month. The booth provides predictable income. From a survival standpoint, you've won.

From a growth standpoint, you've stopped moving.

This is why plateaus are hardest to break after you've been selling for years. The longer you operate within a structure, the more normal it feels. The more normal it feels, the harder it is to imagine doing something fundamentally different. Comfort doesn't announce itself as danger—it presents itself as wisdom.

But comfort is not neutral.

It actively discourages the kind of questioning growth requires. It convinces you that the risk isn't worth it, that the upside is uncertain, that the timing isn't right. It whispers that stability is rare and should be protected at all costs.

What it doesn't tell you is that stagnation is also a cost.

Comfort slowly trades future potential for present ease. It keeps income flat while expenses creep upward. It dulls creativity. It turns the booth into something you manage rather than something you're building toward.

And because nothing breaks, you don't notice what's being lost.

The truth is this: staying comfortable is a choice. Not a failure. Not a flaw. A choice.

But it's a choice that should be made consciously—not by default.

Recognizing comfort as a risk doesn't mean you should abandon everything that works. It means you should be willing to challenge it. Growth doesn't require recklessness, but it does require disruption. And disruption always feels uncomfortable before it feels productive.

If you've been stuck on a plateau, it's not because you did something wrong. It's because you did enough things right to get comfortable—and then stopped questioning what that comfort was costing you.

The Plateau Is a Signal, Not a Verdict

The most important thing to understand about a vendor plateau is that it is not a judgment.

It is not the market telling you that you've reached your limit. It is not proof that you're bad at this, that your booth has peaked, or that growth is no longer possible for you. A plateau doesn't mean you've failed—it means the current version of your booth has finished teaching you what it can.

That distinction changes everything.

When a booth reaches equilibrium, it's sending information. Sales have stabilized because the structure has stabilized. The inventory mix, price bands, layout, and customer expectations are all aligned. Nothing is broken. Nothing is misfiring. The system is simply operating exactly as designed.

If you don't like the outcome, the design—not the effort—has to change.

This is where many vendors get stuck emotionally. They treat the plateau as something to endure rather than something to interpret. They wait it out, hoping the market will shift or foot traffic will improve enough to push them through it. Sometimes that happens temporarily—but without structural change, the ceiling returns.

Because ceilings don't dissolve on their own.

Plateaus exist to signal readiness. They appear when a booth has matured past incremental gains. When tweaking no longer works. When maintenance replaces momentum. They are an invitation to reconfigure—not to quit.

The vendors who eventually break through are not the ones who hustle harder. They're the ones who listen more carefully. They stop asking how to sell *more of the same* and start asking what the booth needs to become in order to earn more.

That question is uncomfortable because it threatens familiarity.

It forces you to reconsider inventory categories you've relied on, pricing strategies you've normalized, and layouts you've stopped noticing. It requires stepping back far enough to see the booth as a system rather than a collection of items. It demands intentional disruption instead of reactive adjustment.

But that discomfort is productive.

Once you recognize a plateau as a signal, the frustration begins to lift. The confusion gains context. You stop blaming yourself or the market and start focusing on design. The problem becomes solvable—not emotionally, but structurally.

This is the turning point.

Staying on a plateau is not a moral failure. Choosing to ignore its message is simply choosing stability over growth. There's nothing inherently wrong with that choice—as long as it's conscious.

But if you want more than maintenance...
If you want progress instead of preservation...
If you want the booth to grow again instead of merely sustain itself...

Then the plateau isn't the end of the road.

It's the sign that you're ready for the next phase.

Chapter Takeaway
Plateaus feel safe because nothing is wrong.
They persist because nothing is challenged.
They break only when structure—not effort—changes.

In the next chapter, we'll examine **how ceilings are actually broken**—not through hustle or guesswork, but through deliberate structural shifts that reset what a booth is capable of producing.

Breaking the Ceiling

Growth Requires Disruption

Ceilings are not broken accidentally.

They don't crack because you worked harder, showed up more consistently, or cared more deeply. They don't give way because you sourced better pieces, cleaned more often, or posted one more time online. Ceilings break only when something fundamental changes—and that change is almost never comfortable.

This is where many vendors get stuck.

After recognizing a plateau, the instinct is to look for *improvements*. Small ones. Safe ones. Adjustments that don't threaten what already works. Vendors tweak pricing slightly. They bring in more inventory. They rearrange shelves and displays. They optimize around the edges of the booth, hoping that enough marginal gains will eventually add up to growth.

They don't.

Incremental improvement works only until a structure is complete. Once a booth has stabilized, small changes stop compounding. They get absorbed. The system adjusts, settles, and returns to equilibrium. The ceiling remains intact.

This is not because the vendor lacks skill or effort. It's because the booth, as a system, is doing exactly what it was designed to do.

That realization is uncomfortable.

Most vendors have been taught—explicitly or implicitly—that growth comes from refinement. From doing the same things better. From polishing what already exists. And in the early stages of booth selling, that belief is rewarded. Refinement *does* lead to progress. Optimization *does* increase returns.

Until it doesn't.

What breaks ceilings is not refinement. It's disruption.

Not chaos. Not recklessness. Not throwing everything out and starting over. Disruption, in this context, means deliberately altering the structure of the booth in a way that forces new behavior—from customers and from the vendor. It means changing the rules the booth operates under, not just playing the game more efficiently.

That distinction matters.

Change is easy to talk about. Vendors change things all the time. They rotate inventory. They shift layouts. They test new categories. But most of these changes happen *within* the same framework. The booth looks different, but it functions the same. Customers browse the same way. They make the same decisions. They spend the same amounts.

Disruption is different.

Disruption alters how customers interact with the booth. It changes where attention goes, how decisions are made, and what feels worth buying. It forces the booth to behave differently—and that's what creates new earning capacity.

This is why ceilings feel so permanent. They are protected by familiarity.

The booth you've built is familiar to you. You know where everything goes. You know what sells. You know what feels safe. Over time, that familiarity becomes invisible. You stop seeing the booth as a system and start seeing it as a collection of items you manage. Decisions become habitual. Assumptions go unchallenged.

And because the booth still works, nothing demands a deeper look.

Breaking a ceiling requires stepping back far enough to see the booth clearly again—not as *yours*, but as a machine producing predictable results. It requires separating identity from outcome. It requires admitting that the version of the booth that got you here may be the very thing holding you in place.

That's not an easy admission.

For many vendors, the idea of disruption feels irresponsible. Risky. Unnecessary. Why gamble with steady income? Why fix what isn't broken? Why invite instability when the booth is paying its way?

Those are reasonable questions. They're also the questions that keep ceilings intact.

The truth is that growth always looks irresponsible from the inside. It threatens routines that feel earned. It challenges decisions you've defended. It introduces uncertainty into systems that feel controlled. But without that disruption, the booth cannot expand—only maintain.

This chapter is not about chasing growth blindly.

It's about understanding *where* growth actually comes from and *why* it has been elusive. It's about identifying the specific levers that raise ceilings—and recognizing why most effort never touches them. It's about learning the difference between being busy and being effective, between change and redesign, between managing a booth and operating one.

Most importantly, this chapter is about permission.

> Permission to disrupt what works.
> Permission to question what feels settled.
> Permission to let go of structures that once served you well.

Because every ceiling you've hit was built by success, not failure. And breaking it doesn't mean you were wrong—it means you're ready for something more.

In the sections that follow, we'll dismantle the belief that more effort equals more growth. We'll identify the structural limits that keep booths stuck. And we'll begin reframing your booth—not as a static space to maintain, but as a system designed to produce results.

Ceilings don't fall on their own.

But once you know how they're built, you can finally decide whether to keep living under them—or tear them down.

Why Incremental Improvements Stop Working

Incremental improvement is how most vendors are taught to grow.

Raise prices a little. Improve displays. Add a few new categories. Tighten sourcing. Post more consistently. Do everything you're already doing—but slightly better. In the early stages of booth selling, this approach works. Small refinements compound because the structure itself is still incomplete. There is room to optimize.

That window eventually closes.

Once a booth reaches maturity, incremental improvements stop producing meaningful gains—not because they're wrong, but because they're operating inside a finished system. At that point, refinements no longer stack. They get absorbed. The booth adjusts, stabilizes, and returns to its baseline.

From the vendor's perspective, this feels confusing and unfair.

You remember a time when small changes mattered. When a better display led to higher sales. When tightening pricing increased margins. When swapping out slow inventory noticeably improved cash flow. That history creates an expectation: *if I just keep improving, growth will come back.*

But what you're really remembering is a different phase of the booth's life.

In early growth, the booth is unfinished. Every improvement fills a gap. Every correction removes friction. Every refinement brings the structure closer to alignment. Results feel responsive because the system is still forming.

Once alignment is achieved, responsiveness disappears.

At that point, incremental change becomes maintenance masquerading as progress. The booth looks more polished, but it doesn't perform differently. Margins stay flat. Sales hover in the same range. Good months and average months trade places, but the average never moves.

This is where vendors misdiagnose the problem.

Instead of recognizing a structural ceiling, they assume the improvements aren't *good enough*. They try harder. They tweak more frequently. They add layers of effort. Ironically, this often makes the booth worse—more cluttered, more confusing, more emotionally exhausting—without raising revenue.

Incremental improvements fail at this stage for one simple reason: they don't change behavior.

Customers shop the booth the same way. They notice the same things. They make the same decisions. They spend the same amounts. The booth may be cleaner, fuller, or better lit—but the experience hasn't shifted.

Growth requires behavior change.

Incremental improvements are designed to optimize existing behavior, not create new outcomes. They assume the current system is fundamentally sound and just needs tuning. When the system itself is the limitation, tuning becomes noise.

This is why so many plateaued vendors feel like they're "doing everything right" while seeing no progress. They are improving within a box that has already defined its limits. The effort is real. The outcome is capped.

Another reason incremental change fails is emotional safety.

Small adjustments feel responsible. They don't threaten income. They don't require letting go of successful inventory. They don't force uncomfortable decisions. Vendors can make them without questioning their identity, taste, or past choices. That safety makes incrementalism appealing—but also ineffective.

Growth, by contrast, feels disruptive because it challenges assumptions.

It asks whether the booth's categories still make sense. Whether price bands are serving the goal or just preserving comfort.

Whether layout choices are intentional or habitual. These questions don't lead to small tweaks—they lead to redesign.

Incremental improvements delay those questions.

They create the illusion of progress while keeping the core structure intact. Vendors feel busy and proactive, which reduces urgency. The plateau becomes tolerable rather than actionable.

This is why breaking a ceiling often feels like a sudden leap rather than a gradual climb. Growth doesn't come from stacking tiny wins forever—it comes from changing the system so that effort produces a different return.

That doesn't mean incremental improvement is useless. It means it has a ceiling of its own.

Once that ceiling is reached, the only way forward is to stop refining and start redesigning. To stop adjusting the edges and start questioning the foundation.

Understanding this is critical, because it reframes failure.

If incremental improvements aren't working anymore, it doesn't mean you've run out of ideas or skill. It means you've exhausted the current structure. The booth is no longer asking for better execution—it's asking for a different design.

And design is where real growth begins.

Structural Levers That Actually Raise a Booth's Ceiling

Once incremental improvements stop working, the instinct is often to assume that growth has become random—dependent on traffic, trends, or timing. In reality, growth hasn't disappeared. It has simply shifted away from the areas most vendors focus on.

Ceilings are not raised by effort. They're raised by leverage.

Structural levers are the elements of a booth that directly influence customer behavior at scale. They determine how attention flows, how decisions are made, and how much money can realistically change hands in the space. Most vendors touch these levers unintentionally, if at all. They focus on inputs—more inventory, more sourcing, more work—while ignoring the mechanics that convert interest into revenue.

Raising a ceiling means changing how the booth functions, not how hard you push it.

The first major lever is inventory role, not inventory category. Most vendors think in terms of *what* they sell. They rarely think in terms of *why* each item exists in the booth. In a high-performing booth, inventory plays distinct roles. Some pieces exist to stop traffic. Others exist to anchor pricing expectations. Some exist purely to convert interest into margin.

When every item is treated the same, the booth becomes flat.

Traffic drivers are not always your best sellers. They are the pieces that create pause—the items that make customers stop, look closer, and step inside the booth. These pieces may be visually striking, unusual, or simply oversized. Their job is attention, not revenue. Without them, customers pass by without engaging.

Margin anchors serve a different function. These are the items that establish value perception. They justify pricing across the booth. When customers see higher-priced, well-presented pieces, mid-range items feel more reasonable. Without anchors, pricing collapses inward, and everything competes in the same narrow band.

Conversion inventory does the real work. These are the pieces that sell consistently because they fit the customer's emotional and financial comfort zone. They don't need to be flashy. They need to be clear. Their job is to turn browsing into buying.

Most plateaued booths blur these roles.

Everything is expected to do everything. Every item needs to attract attention, justify its price, and convert. That's unrealistic—and it caps performance. Assigning clear roles to inventory changes how the booth operates, even without adding a single new item.

The second lever is price band structure.

Many booths technically have a range of prices, but functionally live in one band. Items may be labeled differently, but they feel similar in value. When this happens, customers stop making comparative decisions. They either buy impulsively or not at all.

Intentional price banding creates movement.

Low-entry items reduce hesitation and create momentum. Mid-range items capture the bulk of sales. Higher-end items slow the customer down and elevate perceived quality. The key is separation—not just in price, but in presentation. When bands blur, ceilings form.

The third lever is density versus breathing room.

Vendors often respond to stagnation by adding more inventory, assuming choice will drive sales. In reality, excess density increases cognitive load. Customers become overwhelmed, decisions slow, and conversion drops.

Breathing room is not wasted space. It's decision space.

High-performing booths use density strategically. They cluster where comparison is useful and create space where emphasis is needed. This guides the customer's eye and reduces friction. Removing items can raise a ceiling faster than adding them.

The fourth lever is visual hierarchy.

Most booths lack a clear focal structure. Everything competes equally for attention, which means nothing wins. Customers scan, feel uncertain, and move on.

Visual hierarchy tells customers where to look first, second, and third. It creates a narrative inside the booth. Without it, shopping becomes work.

Hierarchy isn't about perfection—it's about dominance. One element must lead. Everything else must support it. When hierarchy is intentional, customer behavior changes immediately.

The final lever is decision friction.

Friction is anything that slows or complicates buying. Confusing pricing. Overlapping categories. Unclear value. Emotional hesitation. Every booth has friction points, but plateaued booths rarely identify or remove them.

Reducing friction doesn't feel dramatic, but its impact is cumulative. Each eliminated hesitation increases conversion slightly. At scale, that difference raises the ceiling.

What makes these levers powerful is that they operate regardless of effort. Once adjusted, they influence every customer who enters the booth. They change outcomes without demanding more work.

This is why some booths outperform others with less inventory, less effort, and less stress. They are structurally aligned. Their systems support sales instead of resisting them.

Raising a ceiling isn't about finding a secret tactic. It's about identifying which levers matter—and finally pulling them.

The Difference Between Rotation and Replacement

Most vendors believe they are refreshing their booth when, in reality, they are preserving it.

Inventory rotates. Shelves get refilled. New pieces arrive. Old ones sell or get moved out. On the surface, the booth appears dynamic. But functionally, nothing changes. Sales remain flat. Customer behavior stays predictable. The ceiling holds.

The reason is simple: rotation maintains structure. Replacement changes it.

Rotation is when new inventory enters the booth but serves the same role as what it replaced. The price band stays the same. The visual impact stays the same. The emotional decision for the customer stays the same. From the system's perspective, nothing new has happened.

Replacement forces the booth to behave differently.

True replacement alters at least one structural lever. It introduces a new price anchor, changes density, shifts visual hierarchy, or reframes how customers move and decide. Replacement doesn't just fill space—it changes expectations.

This is where many vendors struggle, not because they don't understand the concept, but because replacement feels risky.

Rotation feels safe. It's familiar. You know how to source within your comfort zone. You know what price ranges move. You know what fits the booth's identity. Replacement, by contrast, requires letting go of inventory that still sells *enough*. It asks you to disrupt categories that aren't broken, just capped.

That distinction matters.

Most plateaued booths are full of inventory that sells occasionally. Very little is truly dead. This creates a false sense of security. If items are moving, even slowly, it feels irresponsible to remove them. Vendors tell themselves they just need more patience, better placement, or the right customer.

Replacement demands a harder question: *Is this item contributing to growth, or just occupying space?*

Answering that question honestly often means removing things that feel "fine." Things that match the booth. Things you like. Things that have always been there. Rotation protects emotional comfort. Replacement challenges it.

Another trap is mistaking novelty for replacement.

New inventory is not automatically new behavior. If the new pieces look, feel, and price the same as what was there before, customers respond the same way. They browse, hesitate, and move on. The booth feels updated but unchanged.

Replacement changes the decision landscape.

It forces customers to reassess value. It introduces contrast. It creates new pauses and new paths. Even small replacements—if they alter role or placement—can have outsized effects.

This is why replacement often feels dramatic after the fact.

Vendors who break ceilings frequently describe a moment when "something clicked" or "everything shifted at once." In reality, what changed was not luck or timing, but structure. A replacement disrupted the system enough to unlock new behavior.

The challenge is that replacement often lowers short-term comfort.

Sales may dip briefly as customers recalibrate. The booth may feel unfamiliar. The vendor may feel exposed. This discomfort is where many people retreat back to rotation, restoring the familiar structure and, with it, the ceiling.

But discomfort is temporary. Ceilings are persistent.

Understanding the difference between rotation and replacement reframes inventory decisions entirely. The question stops being "What should I bring in next?" and becomes "What does the booth need to become in order to grow?"

That shift is uncomfortable—and essential.

Rotation keeps a booth alive. Replacement allows it to evolve.

Intentional Risk vs Reckless Change
One of the biggest reasons vendors hesitate to break a ceiling is fear—specifically, fear of doing something *wrong*.

After years of building stability, risk starts to feel irresponsible. The booth pays its way. Income is predictable. Mistakes feel costly now in a way they didn't at the beginning. So when growth stalls, vendors don't think, *What needs to change?* They think, *What can I safely adjust without breaking anything?*

That mindset protects the booth—but it also traps it.

There's an important distinction most vendors never make: the difference between reckless change and intentional risk.

Reckless change is reactionary

It's driven by frustration, boredom, or panic. Vendors overhaul everything at once. They abandon categories without understanding why they worked. They chase trends that don't align with their customer base. They make emotional decisions and hope something sticks. When results don't improve immediately, they retreat, convinced that risk doesn't work.

Intentional risk is the opposite.

Intentional risk is deliberate, contained, and informed. It's based on understanding the system well enough to know *which* lever to pull and *why*. It doesn't gamble the entire booth—it challenges one constraint at a time.

Most vendors avoid intentional risk because it still *feels* dangerous.

That's because intentional risk threatens certainty. It introduces unknowns into a system that has become predictable. Even when the math makes sense, the emotional cost feels high. You are choosing to disrupt something that works in order to build something that might work better.

That leap is uncomfortable by design.

Intentional risk starts with clarity.

You don't change everything. You identify the specific structural limit holding the booth back. Is it price compression? Is it visual noise? Is it inventory role confusion? Is it decision friction? Once the constraint is clear, the risk becomes targeted.

For example, replacing an entire category is reckless if you don't understand its function. But replacing one role within that category—such as removing low-margin fillers to introduce a stronger price anchor—is intentional. The booth still functions, but its behavior shifts.

The goal is not volatility. The goal is response.

Intentional risk always asks: *What behavior am I trying to change?*
Reckless change asks: *What do I feel like changing?*

Another key difference is containment.

Intentional risk is bounded. You decide in advance what success looks like, how long you'll test the change, and what metrics matter. You give the system time to respond. Reckless change reacts emotionally to short-term outcomes and abandons strategy too quickly.

This is where many vendors misjudge risk.

They try something new, feel uncomfortable, see temporary uncertainty, and interpret that as failure. In reality, the booth is recalibrating. Customers are adjusting. The system is learning. Pulling back too soon restores the old ceiling and reinforces the belief that change doesn't work.

Intentional risk requires patience.

Not blind patience—measured patience. Long enough to gather feedback, not so long that inertia returns. This balance is difficult, especially for vendors who rely on booth income. But it's also the only way growth happens without chaos.

Another misconception is that intentional risk requires confidence.
It doesn't.

It requires understanding.

Confidence comes later—after the system responds. Before that, uncertainty is normal. Vendors who break ceilings aren't fearless. They're willing to tolerate discomfort because they trust the process more than the feeling.

The irony is that staying on a plateau is not risk-free.

Flat income in a rising-cost environment is a slow loss. Comfort hides erosion. What feels stable today may be less viable tomorrow. Intentional risk is often safer than passive stagnation—it just doesn't feel that way in the moment.

Breaking a ceiling is not about being bold for the sake of boldness. It's about being honest about what the booth needs.

It's about accepting that growth always looks risky before it looks inevitable.

Once you understand the difference between reckless change and intentional risk, fear becomes information instead of a stop sign.

And that's when real redesign can begin.

Redesigning the Booth as a System

Breaking a ceiling permanently requires a shift in how you *see* your booth.

As long as the booth is viewed as a collection of items—things to source, price, and arrange—growth will always be accidental. You may get lucky. You may catch a trend. You may have a strong season. But sustainable expansion only happens when the booth is treated as a system.

A system has inputs, flow, friction, and output. It behaves predictably. It produces consistent results. And when results stall, the solution isn't to work harder—it's to redesign the system.

Most vendors never make this shift. They remain curators long after their booth demands an operator.

The Booth Is Not a Collection — It's a Machine

Collections are static. Systems are dynamic.

When you think in collections, decisions are emotional and item-based. *Do I like this? Does it fit my style? Will someone eventually buy it?* These questions matter—but they don't scale. They don't explain why two booths with similar inventory perform wildly differently.

Machines, on the other hand, are built for outcomes.

A high-performing booth is engineered to produce sales through predictable customer behavior. It doesn't rely on taste alone. It relies on sequencing, contrast, and decision clarity. Items are not present because they're interesting—they're present because they perform a function.

This is why some booths feel intentional even when they're imperfect. You can sense structure. There's a rhythm to how you move through them. Your attention is guided. Your decisions feel easier.

That isn't luck. It's system design.

Inputs: Inventory as Fuel, Not Decoration

In a system, inventory is fuel.

What you bring into the booth matters far less than *why* it's there. High-level vendors assign roles to inventory whether they realize it or not. Plateaued vendors treat all inventory as equal, which flattens performance.

There are three core roles inventory plays inside a system:

Traffic drivers exist to stop movement. They create pause. Their job is to interrupt the aisle and pull customers in. These pieces are often visually dominant or unusually scaled. They may not sell often—and that's fine. Their value is attention.

Margin anchors exist to frame value. These are higher-priced, well-presented items that make everything else feel more reasonable. Without anchors, customers default to price sensitivity. With anchors, they evaluate comparatively.

Conversion inventory exists to close. These are the pieces customers feel safe buying. They're clear, accessible, and emotionally justified. This category does most of the financial work.

When inventory roles are unclear, the booth becomes noisy. Customers browse but hesitate. Nothing stands out long enough to matter. Sales flatten not because inventory is bad—but because it's misassigned.

Fuel without intention creates drag.

Flow: How Customers Move, Pause, and Decide

Flow is the most misunderstood element of booth design.

Vendors imagine customers browsing freely, but in reality, movement follows patterns. People slow down at visual breaks. They hesitate at decision clusters. They disengage when overwhelmed.

A system-designed booth anticipates this.

Flow begins before the customer enters the space. What they see from the aisle determines whether they step in at all. Once inside, pathing determines whether they linger or retreat. Every pause point should be intentional. Every bottleneck should serve a purpose.

When flow is ignored, customers feel subconsciously uncomfortable. They skim instead of explore. They exit without realizing why.

Good flow reduces cognitive load. It helps customers make one decision at a time instead of all of them at once.

That clarity raises ceilings.

Friction: Where Sales Quietly Die

Friction is anything that creates hesitation.

Most vendors think of friction as pricing alone. In reality, friction exists everywhere. Unclear categories. Inconsistent presentation. Visual clutter. Emotional uncertainty. Even physical discomfort.

The danger of friction is that it doesn't stop customers outright— it slows them just enough to kill momentum.

Each hesitation compounds.

Customers think *maybe later*. They tell themselves they'll come back. They move on. The sale disappears without resistance or feedback.

System redesign requires actively hunting friction.

Where do customers pause too long?
Where do they pick things up and put them back?
Where do they look confused rather than curious?

Removing friction rarely feels dramatic. It feels like subtraction. Fewer items. Cleaner groupings. Clearer pricing. More breathing room.

But friction removal is one of the fastest ways to raise conversion without adding inventory or effort.

Conversion: Turning Attention Into Money

Attention is not value. Conversion is.

Many booths attract interest but fail to translate it into sales. Customers admire, comment, and move on. Vendors mistake compliments for success.

A system is designed to assist decisions.

This means reducing the emotional work required to say yes. Clear pricing. Obvious use cases. Visual cues that suggest ownership. Customers should feel guided, not pressured.

Conversion improves when customers understand *why* something belongs in their life—not just why it's nice.

High-performing booths don't rely on hope. They rely on clarity.

Operators Think in Systems, Not Objects

This is the final shift—and the most important.

Vendors think in items. Operators think in outcomes.

Operators measure performance by behavior, not feelings. They observe how customers interact with the space. They adjust structure based on response, not preference. They are willing to let go of inventory that doesn't serve the system—even if it sells occasionally.

This mindset removes emotion from decision-making without removing care.

It allows the booth to evolve.

When you redesign the booth as a system, ceilings stop feeling mysterious. You can see where limits form and why. You can identify which lever to pull next. Growth becomes intentional instead of accidental.

That's the difference between maintaining a booth and operating one.

And once you see your booth as a system, you can never unsee it.

Chapter Takeaway
You Can't Grow Without Letting Go

Every ceiling you've hit was built by a version of you that succeeded.

That matters, because it reframes what comes next. The structure you're being asked to disrupt isn't a mistake—it's proof that you did something right. The booth stabilized because your decisions worked. The plateau exists because the system reached equilibrium.

But equilibrium is not the same thing as potential.

Growth does not come from preserving what once worked. It comes from releasing it—carefully, intentionally, and without resentment. That's the part most vendors struggle with. Letting go feels like erasing effort. Like admitting that past decisions are now liabilities. Like betraying the booth you worked so hard to build.

That interpretation is understandable—and wrong.

Letting go is not rejection. It's progression.

Every structural redesign requires loss. Categories are removed. Inventory roles change. Price bands shift. Layouts evolve.

Something familiar disappears to make room for something more capable. That loss is not accidental—it's the cost of expansion.

What stalls vendors is not the difficulty of redesign. It's the emotional attachment to what feels earned.

The truth is simple and uncomfortable: you cannot grow into something new while holding onto everything old. Ceilings are reinforced by familiarity. They stay intact because comfort feels like safety. And safety, while valuable, has a price.

Breaking a ceiling means accepting temporary uncertainty in exchange for long-term capacity. It means choosing controlled discomfort over passive stagnation. It means trusting structure over habit, observation over assumption, and design over instinct.

That choice is not mandatory.

You can stay where you are. Many vendors do. Stability is not failure. Maintenance is not shameful. But growth requires a different posture—one that allows space for change, even when that change feels disruptive.

This chapter was not about tactics. It was about perspective.

Once you see your booth as a system, once you understand how ceilings form and why effort alone cannot break them, you gain something more valuable than answers—you gain clarity. You stop fighting the booth and start reshaping it.

And clarity changes everything.

Looking Ahead

In the next chapter, we'll move from redesign to expansion—examining how successful vendors leverage what they've rebuilt to scale intelligently, without losing control or burning out.

Because breaking the ceiling is only the beginning.

What you do after it falls determines how far you go.

Scaling Without Losing Control

Growth Is Where Vendors Get Reckless

Growth is the phase that ends more vendor businesses than struggle ever does.

Struggle forces discipline. It keeps decisions tight. It makes vendors cautious, observant, and intentional. Every purchase is weighed. Every adjustment matters. When money is tight, clarity tends to sharpen.

Growth does the opposite.

When sales increase, pressure eases. Confidence rises. The booth starts producing more than expected, and that success creates a dangerous illusion: that momentum will forgive mistakes. Vendors assume that because things are finally working, they have room to experiment freely, to expand quickly, to say yes without consequence.

This is where things begin to unravel.

Breaking a ceiling feels like permission. Permission to add more inventory. Permission to chase new categories. Permission to take on more space, more commitments, more ideas. Vendors mistake momentum for durability and confuse short-term response with long-term stability.

What they don't realize is that growth doesn't soften systems—it amplifies them.

Any inefficiency that existed before now carries more weight. Any lack of discipline becomes more expensive. Any structural weakness that was tolerable at a lower volume becomes dangerous at a higher one. Growth doesn't hide problems. It magnifies them.

This is why so many vendors experience the same cycle.

> They plateau.
> They break through.
> Sales jump.
> Confidence spikes.

Complexity explodes.
Margins shrink.
Stress returns—worse than before.

From the outside, it looks like bad luck or burnout. From the inside, it feels like betrayal. *I finally fixed the booth—why does it feel harder now?*

The answer is almost always the same: growth happened faster than control.

Scaling without structure is not progress. It's acceleration without steering.

This chapter exists to prevent that mistake.

Not by slowing ambition—but by redefining it.

Scaling does not mean bigger. It does not mean louder. It does not mean constant expansion. Real scale increases output **without increasing strain**. It creates capacity instead of chaos. It makes the booth easier to manage, not harder. Calmer, not noisier.

That kind of growth requires discipline at the exact moment discipline feels unnecessary.

Most vendors abandon their systems right after rebuilding them. They loosen standards. They stop protecting clarity. They trade intentionality for speed. Growth becomes reactive instead of strategic.

And when that happens, the booth doesn't collapse immediately.

It degrades quietly.

Cash flow tightens even as sales rise. Inventory piles up in the wrong places. Restocking turns frantic. The booth feels heavier, messier, louder. Vendors tell themselves this is just the price of success—until exhaustion sets in and the gains evaporate.

This chapter is about stopping that slide before it starts.

It's about recognizing that the moment after a breakthrough is the most dangerous phase of all. It's about learning to scale **without losing the system you just fought to build**. It's about understanding that growth should simplify decisions, not multiply them.

If success has recently found you—or if you're approaching it— this chapter is your guardrail.

Because the goal was never to build a booth that *sells more*.

The goal was to build one that can handle success without breaking itself.

Why Most Vendors Break Through... Then Break Down

The moment a ceiling breaks, most vendors feel relief before they feel danger.

Sales increase. Inventory moves faster. The booth finally responds again. After months—or years—of stagnation, progress feels validating. The struggle appears to be over. Vendors assume the hardest part is behind them.

In reality, they've just entered the most vulnerable phase of the business.

Breakthroughs create emotional momentum long before they create structural resilience. Vendors feel energized, confident, and justified. The booth is finally "working," which makes restraint feel unnecessary. The discipline that carried them through stagnation starts to loosen—not because they intend to abandon it, but because success makes vigilance feel excessive.

This is where breakdown begins.

The first shift is subtle. Vendors start saying yes more easily. Yes to additional inventory. Yes to new categories. Yes to experimenting outside the system they just rebuilt. Each yes feels small and harmless in isolation. After all, sales are up. The booth can "handle it."

But systems don't break from one bad decision. They erode from accumulated compromises.

Growth creates options, and options create temptation. Vendors mistake opportunity for obligation. They assume that because something *could* work, it *should* be tried. The booth, once carefully structured, starts absorbing complexity again.

At the same time, expectations change.

Once sales rise, vendors mentally spend the money before it's earned. They commit to higher sourcing costs. They assume increased volume will cover inefficiencies. They expand based on projected income instead of proven capacity. When reality lags expectation—even slightly—stress returns.

The emotional whiplash is severe.

During the plateau, frustration came from stagnation. After the breakthrough, frustration comes from overload. Vendors feel busier than ever, yet less in control. The booth sells more, but managing it feels harder. The clarity gained during redesign begins to blur.

This is when vendors misinterpret the problem.

They assume the breakdown means they scaled *too much*, when in fact they scaled *without discipline*. They added weight instead of capacity. They expanded complexity instead of reinforcing systems.

Another contributor is misplaced confidence.

Success breeds certainty. Vendors begin trusting instinct again instead of structure. They override systems with intuition. They relax standards that once felt critical. "It's working now" becomes justification for inconsistency.

That confidence isn't arrogance—it's relief.

After long periods of effort without reward, success feels like proof that you finally figured it out. But what actually worked was not instinct or hustle—it was discipline. When that discipline erodes, so does the breakthrough.

The final piece of the breakdown cycle is silence.

As long as sales are still higher than before, vendors ignore warning signs. Tight cash flow is dismissed as temporary. Inventory clutter is framed as abundance. Stress is rationalized as growth pain. The booth hasn't failed yet, so nothing feels urgent.

By the time urgency returns, damage is already done.

This is why so many vendors end up worse off after a breakthrough than before it. They don't fail because growth was wrong—they fail because growth arrived without guardrails. They dismantle the very systems that created success, assuming those systems are no longer necessary.

Understanding this cycle is critical.

Breaking through is not the finish line. It's the moment when discipline matters most. The vendors who sustain success are not the most aggressive—they're the most restrained. They protect structure even when momentum tempts them to abandon it.

Growth is not dangerous because it happens.

It's dangerous because of what it convinces you to stop doing.

Scale Is Capacity, Not Size

Most vendors misunderstand what scaling actually means because they've been conditioned to associate growth with physical expansion.

> More inventory.
> More categories.
> More square footage.
> More movement.

After a breakthrough, these things feel logical. Sales increase, so the natural response is to feed that momentum. If the booth is selling more, it must be able to *hold* more. If customers are buying, the solution must be to give them more choices.

That logic feels intuitive—and it's wrong.

Size creates visibility. Capacity creates control.

Scaling is not about how much you add to the booth. It's about how much the booth can process without degrading. True scale increases output while *reducing strain*. It allows the booth to absorb higher demand without requiring more decisions, more labor, or more emotional energy from you.

When vendors scale by size alone, they add weight without adding strength.

The booth becomes heavier to manage. Restocking takes longer. Pricing becomes harder to track. Visual clarity erodes. What once felt intentional now feels busy. Vendors respond by spending more time in the booth, thinking that effort will compensate for overload.

It doesn't.

Capacity is invisible, which is why it's often ignored.

Capacity is the booth's ability to:

- Guide customer decisions without confusion
- Move inventory without clogging space
- Maintain pricing discipline at higher volume
- Absorb sales spikes without panic sourcing
- Operate predictably without constant intervention

A booth with real capacity feels calm even when it's busy. Customers don't feel rushed or overwhelmed. Vendors don't feel reactive. Systems do the work.

This is why some smaller booths outperform larger ones month after month.

They aren't constrained by space—they're empowered by design. Their inventory roles are clear. Their price bands are intentional. Their layout reduces friction instead of creating it. Customers move through the booth naturally and make decisions with less hesitation.

The booth doesn't fight demand. It processes it.

When vendors confuse scale with size, they introduce several predictable failures.

The first is decision overload.

As inventory increases without structure, customers are forced to compare too many similar options. Instead of choosing, they stall. Instead of buying, they browse. Conversion drops even as interest rises. Vendors mistake this for a traffic problem when it's actually a capacity issue.

The second failure is operational drag.

More inventory requires more tracking, more pricing, more maintenance, and more emotional energy. The booth becomes harder to manage precisely when it should be getting easier. Vendors feel busy but less effective. Growth begins to feel like punishment.

The third failure is false security.

Higher sales numbers create confidence, but that confidence is often built on unstable foundations. Cash flow tightens because inventory dollars are tied up longer. Margins compress because clarity is lost. Vendors assume volume will fix these issues later.

It rarely does.

Capacity-focused scaling avoids these traps by asking a different question.

Instead of What can I add? the question becomes:
What can this system reliably handle without friction?

That question changes behavior immediately.

It encourages vendors to remove obstacles before adding load. It prioritizes clarity over variety. It values predictability over excitement. It treats growth as something to be *absorbed*, not chased.

A booth designed with capacity in mind often looks restrained on the surface. Fewer categories. Clearer pricing. More intentional spacing. Less noise. To an outsider, it may even look conservative.

But internally, it's powerful.

When demand increases, nothing breaks. Restocking follows established rules. Inventory roles remain intact. Decisions don't multiply—they simplify. The booth scales quietly, without drama.

This is the kind of growth that lasts.

It's also the kind most vendors never experience because it requires resisting the urge to expand physically when momentum hits. It requires trusting structure over excitement. It requires believing that *restraint is not stagnation*.

Scale is not about how much the booth contains.

It's about how much pressure it can handle without losing itself.

Once you understand that, growth stops feeling urgent—and starts feeling intentional.

Leverage: Adding Output Without Adding Weight

Leverage is what separates growth that compounds from growth that collapses.

Most vendors assume leverage comes from working harder or sourcing smarter. They believe output increases only when effort increases. That assumption holds early on—when the booth is small, simple, and forgiving. But once scale enters the picture, effort becomes an unreliable tool.

Leverage is about getting more results from the *same* structure.

In a leveraged booth, sales increase without proportional increases in time, stress, or decision-making. The system does more work so the vendor doesn't have to. This is why leverage feels calm when it's working and overwhelming when it's missing.

The first form of leverage is inventory efficiency.

Not all inventory carries the same weight. Some items require constant attention. Others quietly perform month after month.

Leveraged booths prioritize pieces that do more work per square foot—items that sell consistently, anchor pricing, or pull customers deeper into the space.

This doesn't mean abandoning character or uniqueness. It means understanding return on attention.

Inventory that demands explanation, rearrangement, or constant justification is expensive—even if it sells occasionally. Inventory that communicates value instantly is efficient. Over time, replacing high-maintenance pieces with high-efficiency ones increases output without increasing workload.

The second form of leverage is price discipline.

Many vendors loosen pricing as sales rise. They assume volume will compensate for thinner margins. This is one of the fastest ways to add weight without adding capacity.

Price discipline is leverage because it stabilizes cash flow and simplifies decisions. When price bands are intentional and defended, vendors don't need to constantly reevaluate or discount. Customers understand value faster. Hesitation decreases. Conversion improves.

Strong pricing systems reduce emotional labor.

Instead of debating each item internally, the booth enforces rules. Items are priced according to role, not mood. That consistency compounds over time, especially as volume increases.

The third form of leverage is visual repetition with intent.

Vendors often mistake repetition for boredom. In reality, repetition creates recognition. Recognition reduces cognitive effort. Cognitive ease increases buying behavior.

Leveraged booths repeat successful patterns deliberately. They reuse layouts that convert. They mirror groupings that sell. They allow customers to recognize structure quickly so attention can shift to product instead of orientation.

This kind of repetition feels boring to the vendor—but powerful to the customer.

The fourth form of leverage is decision reduction.
Every decision you remove from the system increases capacity.

Clear categories reduce browsing fatigue. Obvious focal points reduce scanning. Consistent pricing reduces hesitation. Each simplification frees cognitive bandwidth for buying.

This is why leveraged booths often look simpler, not busier. They aren't trying to impress—they're trying to convert.

The final form of leverage is **constraint**.

Constraints feel limiting, but they focus energy. When vendors limit categories, price bands, or sourcing rules, they reduce noise. That clarity allows the booth to perform predictably at higher volume.

Without constraint, growth becomes reactive. With constraint, growth becomes scalable.

Leverage is not flashy. It doesn't announce itself. It quietly reshapes how effort translates into results.

When leverage is present, growth feels lighter. When it's missing, growth feels heavier no matter how much money is coming in.

Understanding leverage prepares you for the most important part of scaling: knowing when to stop.

Warning Signs You're Growing Too Fast
Growth almost never feels like a threat when it begins.

It feels like relief. Like validation. Like proof that the work you put in during the plateau finally paid off. Sales increase, inventory moves faster, and the booth feels alive again. Vendors tell themselves they're finally on the other side of the hard part.

That belief is what makes this phase so dangerous.

Growing too fast does not announce itself with failure. It announces itself with momentum. The booth looks successful, deposits are larger, and activity increases. On the surface, everything points in the right direction. Underneath, however, the system is being asked to carry more weight than it was designed for.

The warning signs are subtle at first. They rarely appear all at once. More often, they show up in layers—emotional, operational, and financial—long before sales numbers reflect a problem. Vendors who miss these signs don't fail because growth was wrong. They fail because they mistake acceleration for stability.

The first and most reliable warning sign is internal.

When Growth Makes the Booth Feel Heavier Instead of Easier
Real scale reduces pressure. Poor scale increases it.

When systems are aligned, higher sales should simplify your role, not complicate it. Decisions should become clearer. Restocking should become more predictable. The booth should begin to operate with less direct intervention from you.

When growth is happening too fast, the opposite occurs.

You feel constantly behind. The booth demands attention instead of responding to it. Tasks pile up instead of resolving themselves. You're busy, but not grounded. Even good sales days feel draining rather than energizing.

This heaviness is often dismissed as "normal growth stress." Vendors assume this is simply what success feels like. They tell themselves they'll adjust once things settle down.

They rarely do.

Over time, heaviness evolves into avoidance. You stop looking at the booth holistically because doing so feels overwhelming. Decisions get postponed. Problems are managed locally instead of structurally. You spend more time reacting to symptoms than addressing causes.

This is not a motivation problem. It's a capacity problem.

When growth adds weight instead of reducing effort, the system is already under strain—even if sales are strong.

When Cash Flow Tightens Even as Sales Increase

This is one of the most deceptive warning signs because it contradicts expectation.

Sales are up. Deposits are larger. From the outside, everything looks better. Yet internally, cash feels tighter. Inventory purchases require more money upfront. Margins feel thinner. You find yourself waiting on the next good weekend to "catch up."

Vendors often blame timing. They assume cash flow will normalize once growth stabilizes. What they're actually experiencing is false prosperity.

As systems degrade, inventory stops cycling efficiently. More dollars sit idle on shelves. Capital gets locked into pieces that take longer to move. Small inefficiencies that didn't matter at lower volume now compound.

Growth masks this problem temporarily.

Higher sales hide slower turns. Bigger deposits obscure shrinking usable cash. Vendors respond by sourcing more aggressively to maintain momentum, unintentionally tightening the loop further.

This is how growth becomes a trap.

Instead of increasing financial flexibility, it reduces it. You are technically selling more, but operating with less margin for error. One slow month suddenly matters far more than it should.

Cash flow tightening during growth is not a timing issue. It's a signal that discipline has slipped and complexity is eating margin quietly.

When Restocking Becomes Reactive Instead of Intentional
In controlled growth, restocking follows rules.

You know what role needs to be filled. You understand why something sold. Inventory enters the booth with purpose. Even when volume increases, the system guides replacement.

When growth is too fast, restocking becomes urgent.

Shelves empty unexpectedly. Gaps appear where they shouldn't. You buy to fill space instead of to serve structure. Availability starts driving decisions instead of design. The question shifts from *What does the booth need?* to *What can I get right now?*

This is system amnesia.

The rules that created success are slowly forgotten under pressure. You compromise "just this once." You justify pieces that don't quite fit because they'll probably sell. Over time, those compromises stack.

The booth begins to drift.

Restocking urgency rewrites standards. Inventory roles blur. The system becomes inconsistent again—not dramatically, but enough to weaken leverage. Customers sense the loss of clarity immediately, even if you don't.

By the time you notice, you're sourcing more frequently while feeling less effective. Growth has turned reactive.

When Systems Start Breaking Under Pressure
Systems don't fail catastrophically. They erode.

Pricing becomes less consistent. Visual hierarchy softens. Categories overlap. Items that once felt intentional now feel misplaced. The booth still sells—but it no longer guides behavior cleanly.

This stage is especially dangerous because it feels survivable.

Customers still browse. Compliments increase. Interest appears strong. Vendors assume the issue is volume or exposure and respond by adding more inventory or widening selection.

In reality, the booth is becoming confusing.

Small inconsistencies multiply. Customers hesitate longer. Decisions stall. Conversion quietly drops. The booth shifts from being decisive to being interesting.

This is the customer confusion cascade.

Nothing is obviously wrong, but nothing feels easy either. The booth is no longer helping customers say yes—it's asking them to work harder to decide. Most don't.

Vendors often misinterpret this as a traffic issue, when it's actually a system integrity issue. Growth didn't cause the breakdown—it revealed how fragile the structure was without discipline.

The False Confidence Phase: When Control Is Lost Without Being Felt

This is the most dangerous stage of all.

Sales are still strong. Momentum is visible. Confidence is high. Vendors feel justified in their decisions because results appear to support them. This is where overcommitment happens.

You trust instinct more than structure. You override systems because "you know what works now." You assume you'll spot problems early enough to fix them later.

This confidence is not arrogance—it's relief.

After struggling through a plateau, success feels earned. The temptation to enjoy it, expand into it, and relax standards is strong. Unfortunately, this is exactly when correction becomes hardest.

Pride delays restraint. Momentum discourages pullbacks. Every signal that suggests slowing down feels irrational when things are "finally working."

This is the point of no return for many vendors.

They take on commitments they can't unwind easily. They add categories that dilute clarity. They expand complexity faster than capacity. When reality catches up, reversing course feels emotionally and financially painful.

What makes this phase so destructive is timing.

By the time discomfort outweighs confidence, the booth is already carrying too much weight. Fixing it now requires loss— inventory removal, category reduction, and financial tightening. Vendors who delay this correction often burn out instead.

Why These Signs Matter

Growing too fast doesn't destroy booths immediately.

It exhausts vendors quietly.

It replaces clarity with noise. Discipline with urgency. Structure with intuition. Vendors don't quit because growth failed—they quit because growth became heavier than stagnation ever was.

These warning signs are not obstacles to push through. They are feedback. They exist to protect what you built.

Growth should feel calmer over time, not louder. More controlled, not more frantic. If the booth feels increasingly demanding as it succeeds, the system is losing ground.

Recognizing these signs early is not pessimism.

It's professionalism.

The Discipline of Saying No

Growth creates more opportunity than most vendors can handle.

This is the paradox few people warn you about. When the booth is struggling, options are limited. You say no by default because you have to. Time, money, and energy force restraint. Decisions are filtered automatically by scarcity.

When the booth starts working, that filter disappears.

Sales improve. Cash flow loosens. Confidence rises. Suddenly, everything feels possible. New inventory ideas surface. New categories seem viable. New sourcing opportunities appear. People suggest things. You notice trends. You see adjacent opportunities you couldn't touch before.

Growth doesn't just increase revenue—it increases noise.

This is where discipline becomes the most important skill you have.

> Not hustle.
> Not creativity.
> Not ambition.

Discipline.

Most vendors believe saying no is about fear or conservatism. In reality, saying no is how systems stay intact under pressure. It's how clarity is preserved. It's how growth compounds instead of collapsing.

The booths that scale successfully are not the ones that try the most things. They are the ones that **protect the few things that work**.

Growth Creates More Opportunities Than You Can Sustain
Success attracts options.

Once your booth starts performing, everything looks viable. Items that didn't quite fit before suddenly seem workable. Marginal ideas feel promising. You notice adjacent categories and think, *If this is selling, maybe that will too.*

This is where most vendors drift.

They assume opportunity is rare and should be seized. They treat every possibility as a chance they might regret passing up. Growth makes restraint feel foolish—especially after a long period of limitation.

But opportunity is not the same as alignment.

Every "maybe" you say yes to pulls the system slightly off center. One extra category doesn't ruin a booth. One pricing exception doesn't destroy discipline. One experimental purchase doesn't collapse structure.

But systems don't fail from one compromise.

They fail from accumulation.

Each yes adds complexity. Each added variable increases decision load. Each small deviation weakens clarity. Over time, the booth stops behaving predictably—not because anything went wrong, but because too much was allowed in.

The danger of growth is not expansion. It's dilution.

Saying No Is a Structural Decision, Not an Emotional One
Vendors often experience guilt around saying no.

They worry they're missing out. They worry they're being too rigid. They worry restraint means they aren't ambitious enough. These feelings are emotional—but the decision to say no should never be.

Saying no is not about fear.

It's about protection.

Every well-designed system has guardrails. These guardrails are not limitations—they are boundaries that allow the system to function at higher capacity. Without them, performance degrades under pressure.

When you say no to inventory that doesn't fit your system, you're not rejecting growth—you're preserving leverage.

When you say no to categories that dilute clarity, you're not being closed-minded—you're defending conversion.

When you say no to opportunities that add weight without capacity, you're not being cautious—you're being intentional.

Discipline is what allows success to last.

The booths that survive long-term success are not the most flexible. They are the most selective.

The Hidden Cost of "Just Trying It"

"Just trying it" is one of the most expensive phrases in booth selling.

It sounds harmless. Low commitment. Reversible. Vendors convince themselves that experimentation is healthy—and it can be, when done within structure.

Most "just trying it" decisions aren't experiments.

They're compromises.

Items are added without clear roles. Categories are introduced without exit criteria. Pricing exceptions are made without rules. Each decision is justified individually, but none are evaluated systemically.

The cost of these decisions is rarely immediate.

Inventory lingers just long enough to justify keeping it. Layouts shift subtly. Visual hierarchy weakens. The booth becomes harder to read. Customers hesitate more often.

Nothing breaks—but nothing sharpens either.

This is how systems lose their edge.

The most dangerous experiments are the ones that never get evaluated. They don't fail dramatically enough to be removed. They don't succeed clearly enough to be optimized. They simply exist—draining clarity, attention, and energy.

Saying no prevents silent erosion.

Protecting the Booth You Rebuilt

Breaking a ceiling requires discipline.

Keeping it broken requires even more.

After redesigning your booth, clarity becomes your most valuable asset. You now understand how structure affects behavior. You see how systems convert attention into money. That understanding must be protected deliberately.

This is where many vendors regress.

They assume the work is done. They loosen standards. They stop enforcing rules. They allow convenience and opportunity to override structure. Slowly, the booth drifts back toward noise.

Protecting your booth means respecting the system even when it feels restrictive.

> It means enforcing pricing discipline even when sales are strong.
> It means limiting categories even when demand appears broad.
> It means removing inventory that doesn't serve the system—even if it sells occasionally.

Discipline is not static.

It must be renewed continuously, especially during success.

Sustainable Growth Is Selective Growth

The most successful booths often look boring on paper.

They don't chase trends aggressively. They don't pivot constantly. They don't expand endlessly. They do fewer things better than everyone else.

This is not a lack of ambition.

It's clarity.

Selective growth compounds because it reinforces systems instead of straining them. Each decision strengthens the structure. Each addition fits a role. Each no makes the yes more powerful.

These booths feel calm.

They aren't frantic. They aren't chaotic. They aren't constantly reinventing themselves. They operate with confidence because they understand their limits—and respect them.

That respect is what allows growth to last.

Discipline Is What Lets Growth Feel Quiet

The final test of scale is emotional.

If growth makes your booth louder, messier, and more stressful, discipline has slipped. If growth makes decisions easier, operations smoother, and outcomes more predictable, discipline is doing its job.

Saying no is not about shrinking possibility.

It's about choosing which possibilities deserve your system.

Without discipline, growth consumes clarity. With discipline, growth deepens it.

Chapter Takeaway

Growth Should Feel Calmer, Not Louder

Real growth has a tone.

It doesn't shout. It doesn't scramble. It doesn't demand constant attention just to keep moving forward. When growth is working the way it should, it feels quieter than expected—more controlled, more predictable, more deliberate.

That calm is not accidental.

It's the result of discipline layered on top of momentum. It's what happens when capacity is built before complexity, when systems are protected instead of abandoned, and when restraint is treated as a strategic tool rather than a limitation.

Most vendors never experience this version of growth because they mistake noise for progress.

They assume expansion should feel hectic. They accept stress as the cost of success. They believe that if things aren't chaotic, they must not be pushing hard enough. Over time, that belief turns growth into a burden rather than a reward.

But scale is not supposed to exhaust you.

When systems are aligned, growth reduces urgency. Decisions get easier instead of harder. The booth begins to respond predictably. You stop chasing outcomes and start managing inputs. Success becomes something you steer—not something that drags you behind it.

That is the difference between expansion and control.

This chapter wasn't about slowing down ambition. It was about redefining it. Ambition without discipline burns itself out. Ambition with structure compounds quietly. The most successful vendors aren't the ones who say yes to everything—they're the ones who know exactly what they're protecting.

If growth has recently found you, this is the moment to pause— not to stop, but to secure what you've built. Protect clarity. Enforce boundaries. Let systems do the heavy lifting. The discipline you maintain now determines whether this phase becomes a foundation or a flash.

And if growth hasn't arrived yet, this chapter still matters.

Because when it does, the habits you build beforehand will decide how far it carries you.

The goal was never to create a booth that simply sells more.

The goal was to create one that can handle success without losing itself.

Looking Ahead

In the next chapter, we'll shift from control to durability—how long-term vendors design booths that don't just grow, but **last**, adapting to markets, seasons, and life changes without constant reinvention.

Growth should not feel louder over time.

It should feel steadier.

That's how you know you're doing it right.

The Booth That Outlasts the Market

Winning Isn't What You Think It Is

Most vendors believe they'll recognize success when it arrives.

They imagine it as a moment—

> a sales record,
> a perfect month,
> a booth so full it feels unstoppable.

But almost every vendor who reaches that point feels something unexpected shortly afterward.

Not relief.
Not pride.

Uncertainty.

Because the moment passes, and the question quietly replaces it:

Is this it?

This is where many experienced vendors make their most damaging decisions—not because they're failing, but because they're unsure how to interpret success once they've achieved it.

> They confuse momentum with obligation.
> They confuse growth with proof.
> They confuse activity with health.

And in doing so, they unknowingly trade stability for pressure.

Winning in booth selling is rarely loud.
It doesn't announce itself.
It doesn't come with a finish line.

Real winning feels quieter than expected.

It feels like:

- fewer emergency restocks

- fewer emotional decisions

- fewer nights wondering if the booth is "still working"

- fewer reactions to every slow week

The booth begins to behave predictably.
Sales patterns repeat.
Inventory turnover stabilizes.
Your decisions stop feeling like guesses and start feeling like confirmations.

That's when many vendors panic.

Because predictability doesn't feel exciting.

And excitement—especially in creative retail—has been mistakenly marketed as the goal.

> So vendors push again.
> They expand too fast.
> They add categories they don't enjoy managing.
> They chase novelty instead of reinforcing systems.
> They trade calm for complexity.

Not because they need to—but because they're afraid that standing still means slipping backward.

This is the trap.

Winning isn't a peak—it's a **plateau you learn to respect**.

A healthy booth doesn't demand constant reinvention.
It doesn't punish you for missing a week.
It doesn't collapse if you step away for a moment.

It absorbs life.

And that is the real measure of success that most vendors never define for themselves.

If your booth requires:

- constant emotional energy
- constant novelty

- constant vigilance
- constant correction

Then it doesn't matter how well it sells—it's fragile.

Fragility is not failure.
But it is unsustainable.

The vendors who last—five, ten, fifteen years—aren't the ones who hustle the hardest.

They're the ones who build booths that keep working **when they're tired, distracted, busy, or simply human**.

This chapter exists to help you recognize when you've already won—and how to protect that win instead of accidentally dismantling it.

Designing for the Vendor You'll Be in Five Years
Most booths are designed for the vendor you *are right now*.

> Your current energy.
> Your current availability.
> Your current enthusiasm.
> Your current tolerance for chaos.

That's fine in the beginning. It's often necessary. Early-stage booths are built on momentum, effort, and responsiveness. You're learning, adjusting, reacting, and iterating in real time. The booth is an extension of your attention.

But what works early becomes dangerous later if it never evolves.

Because the vendor you are today is not the vendor you'll be five years from now.

Five years from now:

- your time will be divided differently
- your priorities will shift
- your patience for constant maintenance will be lower
- your appetite for risk will be more selective

And if your booth is still demanding the same level of effort it did in year one, resentment starts to creep in.

This is where burnout doesn't look dramatic—it looks quiet.

> You stop enjoying restocks.
> You dread booth visits instead of looking forward to them.
> You feel guilty for not "doing enough," even though the booth is profitable.

That guilt is a signal—not of laziness, but of misalignment.

A durable booth is one that matures alongside its owner.

Designing for the future version of yourself requires a shift in thinking:
You stop asking *"What can I do?"*
and start asking *"What must this booth handle without me?"*

That question changes everything.

> It changes how you select inventory.
> It changes how tightly you curate.
> It changes how much visual complexity you allow.
> It changes how often you're willing to intervene.

The goal is not neglect.
The goal is **forgiveness**.

A forgiving booth is one that doesn't punish you for being human.

It doesn't collapse if you miss a week.
It doesn't look empty if you delay a restock.
It doesn't lose its identity because one item sells unexpectedly fast.

Forgiveness is engineered, not accidental.

It starts with category discipline.

When vendors build booths that rely on constant novelty, rare finds, or one-of-a-kind treasures to carry performance, they also build fragility into the system. Those booths feel impressive—but they require perfect timing, constant sourcing, and emotional investment that's difficult to sustain long-term.

Durable booths lean into:

- repeatable inventory types
- predictable price bands
- categories that replenish easily
- items that sell steadily, not spectacularly

That doesn't mean boring.
It means dependable.

Dependability frees your attention.

It also changes how you stock.

Instead of asking, *"Will this sell?"*
You begin asking, *"Will this still make sense if I don't touch the booth for three weeks?"*

That single question filters out a surprising amount of inventory.

> Fragile items fail this test.
> High-maintenance items fail this test.
> Visually dependent items fail this test.

What remains are items that carry themselves.

The same principle applies to layout.

Booths designed for short-term excitement often rely on tight spacing, layered storytelling, and visual density that requires frequent correction. They look great—until one piece sells. Then the whole composition unravels.

A future-proof booth anticipates disruption.

> It assumes things will sell.
> It assumes gaps will appear.
> It assumes hands will move things slightly out of place.
> It assumes you won't always be there to fix it.

So it builds in:

- breathing room

- visual redundancy
- multiple focal points instead of one perfect centerpiece

These booths don't look "ruined" when something sells.
They look active.

That distinction matters.

A booth that looks active signals health to customers—even during slower weeks. A booth that looks damaged or incomplete creates subconscious hesitation.

Designing for your future self also means being honest about what you want this booth to *do* for you.

Not what you want it to *prove*.

Many vendors unintentionally trap themselves by tying their identity to their booth's performance. Every slow week feels personal. Every change feels risky. Every decision carries emotional weight.

That is exhausting.

A durable booth is emotionally lighter because it is structurally stronger.

> You trust it.
> You understand it.
> You know what it does well—and what it doesn't need to do at all.

That clarity allows you to step back without fear.

And that is the real gift of designing for the vendor you'll be in five years:
freedom without abandonment.

You're not walking away from your booth.
You're building something that doesn't need to be constantly carried.

The most successful long-term vendors aren't the most involved day-to-day.

They're the most intentional up front.

They design systems that age well—because they planned for the day when effort would no longer be abundant.

The Hidden Cost of Constant Optimization

Optimization sounds responsible.

It feels disciplined.
It feels professional.
It feels like what serious vendors *should* be doing.

Tweak the layout.
Adjust the pricing.
Refresh the color palette.
Rotate inventory more aggressively.
Test new categories.

On paper, constant optimization looks like progress.

In practice, it often becomes the quiet force that erodes confidence, stability, and long-term performance.

Because optimization, when applied without restraint, trains you to distrust anything that isn't immediately improving.

Every slow week becomes a problem to solve.
Every flat month becomes evidence something is "wrong."
Every plateau becomes a threat instead of a signal.

And over time, this mindset rewires how you interpret your booth.

Instead of seeing a stable system, you see a fragile one that must be constantly corrected.

That's not optimization.
That's anxiety disguised as strategy.

The truth most vendors don't want to hear is this:

A booth that needs constant optimization is not optimized.

Healthy systems stabilize.
They repeat.
They create patterns.

If your booth only performs when you're actively adjusting it, then you don't have a system—you have a reaction loop.

Reaction loops are exhausting.

They keep you busy without making you safer.
They create activity without creating security.
They reward effort instead of structure.

And worst of all, they make it impossible to tell what's actually working—because nothing is left alone long enough to prove itself.

This is where experienced vendors accidentally sabotage themselves.

They know more.
They see more.
They notice subtleties newer vendors miss.

But instead of using that awareness to reinforce what's already working, they use it to justify constant change.

More data does not always lead to better decisions.
Sometimes it just increases noise.

The booth becomes a laboratory instead of a storefront.
The customer becomes a variable instead of a participant.
The experience becomes unstable—even if sales remain acceptable.

There's also a psychological cost that rarely gets discussed.

When you're always optimizing, you're always implying that the current state is insufficient.

That creates a low-grade dissatisfaction that never resolves.

You don't celebrate wins—you prepare for their disappearance.

You don't trust consistency—you wait for it to fail.
You don't rest—you hover.

Over time, that erodes confidence in your own judgment.

You stop knowing whether something worked because it worked—or because you intervened at just the right moment. The booth stops teaching you, because you never let it finish speaking.

This is especially dangerous for vendors who are already successful.

Optimization has diminishing returns.
The closer you are to a stable system, the more each change risks undoing something you can't immediately see.

The goal is not to stop improving.
The goal is to **earn periods of non-intervention**.

Non-intervention is not neglect.
It's a deliberate strategy.

>It means choosing to observe instead of adjust.
>It means allowing patterns to complete.
>It means resisting the urge to "fix" something that isn't broken simply because you're capable of doing so.

Durable vendors optimize in waves, not constantly.

>They make a change.
>They let it settle.
>They watch for confirmation—not excitement.
>They wait long enough to understand impact.

And then they stop touching it.

That pause is where clarity returns.

You begin to recognize which improvements actually matter—and which ones were just movement for movement's sake.

You also begin to trust your booth again.

Trust is what allows durability.
Durability is what allows longevity.

Longevity is what turns booth selling from a grind into a sustainable part of your life.

Constant optimization feels productive.
But stability is what keeps you in the game.

Durability Is the Advantage No One Teaches

No one teaches durability because it isn't flashy.

> It doesn't photograph well.
> It doesn't spike engagement.
> It doesn't make for exciting advice in online groups.

Durability doesn't look like success in motion—it looks like success at rest.

That's why so many vendors overlook it until they're exhausted, frustrated, or quietly thinking about walking away from something that once felt promising.

But durability is the difference between vendors who *cycle through* the market and vendors who **outlast it**.

> The market will change.
> Trends will rotate.
> Platforms will rise and fall.
> Foot traffic will fluctuate.
> Algorithms will rewrite the rules without warning.

Durable booths absorb these changes instead of reacting violently to them.

> They don't chase every shift.
> They don't panic at every dip.
> They don't rebuild themselves every season.

They bend, then return to form.

Durability is not about resisting change—it's about being structured enough that change doesn't threaten your foundation.

That foundation is built on a few quiet decisions most vendors never make intentionally.

First, durable vendors decide what *doesn't* belong in their booth.

> Not every profitable item deserves a place.
> Not every trend deserves attention.
> Not every opportunity deserves a yes.

Durability requires subtraction.

The longer you sell, the more tempting it becomes to accumulate complexity. New categories, new price tiers, new sourcing channels, new display styles—each addition feels reasonable on its own.

Together, they create fragility.

> Durable booths are opinionated.
> They are selective.
> They say no more often than yes.

That selectivity is what allows them to stay coherent even when conditions shift.

Second, durable vendors define success in a way that doesn't punish them for living.

> They don't require constant growth to feel validated.
> They don't interpret flat periods as failure.
> They don't equate busyness with worth.

> They know their numbers.
> They understand their averages.
> They recognize when performance is within normal variance instead of assuming every deviation needs intervention.

That perspective protects their energy.

Energy is a finite resource.
So is attention.
So is care.

Durable vendors spend those resources where they actually move the needle—and guard them everywhere else.

Third, durable booths are designed to survive interruptions.

> Illness.
> Family obligations.
> Burnout.
> Life events.
> Even simple fatigue.

A booth that collapses the moment you step back is not a business—it's a dependency.

Durable booths anticipate absence.

> They don't rely on perfect timing.
> They don't rely on constant restocking.
> They don't rely on emotional motivation.

They rely on structure.

Structure is the invisible advantage that compounds quietly over time.

It shows up as:

- consistent visual identity

- stable inventory rhythms

- repeatable pricing logic

- predictable customer behavior

These things don't feel exciting.
But they feel safe.

And safety is what allows you to keep going when enthusiasm inevitably dips.

Durability also changes how you relate to the market emotionally.

> You stop feeling personally attacked by slow weeks.
> You stop tying your worth to daily sales.
> You stop interpreting every change as a threat.

The market becomes something you operate within—not something you fight.

That emotional distance is not detachment.
It's maturity.

> It's the difference between reacting and responding.
> Between scrambling and adjusting.
> Between burning out and staying in control.

Most importantly, durability gives you choice.

> You can expand—or not.
> You can downsize—or not.
> You can pivot—or not.
> You can pause—or not.

Because your booth is not held together by urgency.

When vendors ask what separates those who last from those who disappear, the answer is rarely talent, taste, or effort.

It's resilience built through design.

Not just physical design—but emotional, operational, and strategic design.

Durability is the advantage no one teaches because it can't be rushed.

> It's earned by doing fewer things better.
> By trusting systems instead of chasing stimulation.
> By valuing sustainability over spectacle.

If you take nothing else from this book, take this:

A booth that supports your life will always outperform one that consumes it.

> That's how vendors outlast markets.
> That's how success becomes something you can actually live with.
> That's how you win—quietly, steadily, and on your own terms.

How to Build a Booth That Is Structurally Durable

Durability is not a personality trait.
It is not discipline.
It is not willpower.

Durability is the result of decisions made *before* pressure shows up.

Most booths fail durability tests long before the vendor realizes they're being tested. Not because the vendor is doing something wrong—but because the booth was never designed to handle strain.

Strain always arrives eventually.

> Sales fluctuate.
> Foot traffic shifts.
> Life interrupts.
> Energy fades.
> Markets tighten.

A durable booth is not one that performs best in perfect conditions. It is one that continues to function when conditions are imperfect—which is most of the time.

To build that kind of booth, you must stop thinking of it as a display and start thinking of it as a system.

Systems either absorb stress—or amplify it.

This section breaks durability down into **five structural pillars**. If even one of these pillars is weak, the booth becomes dependent on your constant involvement. If all five are present, the booth begins to carry itself.

Pillar 1 — Inventory That Carries Its Own Weight

Durable booths are not carried by hero items.

They are carried by *boring consistency*.

Hero items feel good. They photograph well. They spike dopamine when they sell. But they are unreliable as a foundation. You cannot plan a system around occasional wins.

Durable booths rely on inventory that:

- sells repeatedly
- replenishes easily
- behaves predictably
- does not require explanation

This does not mean low-value or low-interest. It means **low-dependence**.

Ask yourself this question for every category you carry:

If I could not source this for 60 days, would my booth suffer or adapt?

If the booth collapses without that category, it's a liability—not an asset.

Durable inventory has three traits:

1. Replacement is simpler than acquisition
If sourcing feels like a hunt, the category is fragile.

2. Pricing does not require justification
If customers must "understand" the item before purchasing, sales will fluctuate with mood and traffic.

3. Volume matters more than uniqueness
Durability is built through repetition, not rarity.

This is why long-term vendors often look less exciting than newer ones. They've already eliminated categories that demanded too much attention for too little return.

Pillar 2 — Visual Structure That Anticipates Loss
Most booths are designed to look good *when full*.

Durable booths are designed to look good *after something sells*.

This distinction is critical.

If your booth visually collapses when one or two items leave, then every sale creates work. Over time, that turns success into a burden.

Durable booths assume disruption.

They build:

- negative space intentionally
- visual redundancy across multiple areas
- repeatable display logic

Instead of one perfect focal point, there are **layers of interest**.

Instead of fragile symmetry, there is **forgiving balance**.

Instead of tightly interlocked arrangements, there are **independent visual units**.

When something sells, the booth still reads as complete.

This allows you to delay intervention without penalty.

A good test:

If three items sell in different parts of the booth today, would it still look intentional tomorrow?

If the answer is no, your layout is brittle.

Pillar 3 — Pricing That Reduces Decision Fatigue
Durable booths reduce the number of decisions you must make—not just the number of decisions customers make.

Complex pricing systems create invisible strain.

If you are constantly:

- recalculating
- second-guessing
- adjusting margins
- reacting to competitors

You are burning energy that does not compound.

Durable booths operate inside **clear pricing bands**.

You know where most items land before you price them.
You know what "normal" looks like.
You know when something is intentionally outside the norm.

This creates calm.

It also allows you to step away without fear that pricing errors will unravel performance.

Durable pricing is:

- consistent
- defensible
- boring

And boring pricing is resilient pricing.

Pillar 4 — Maintenance Rhythms, Not Maintenance Pressure
Fragile booths rely on urgency.

Durable booths rely on rhythm.

Urgency says:
"I have to fix this now."

Rhythm says:
"This will be addressed during the next cycle."

Durable vendors define:

- how often they restock
- how often they rework layout
- how often they evaluate categories

And then they **honor those intervals**.

This prevents emotional decision-making.

It also prevents the booth from training you to panic every time something shifts slightly off expectation.

If everything is always urgent, nothing is sustainable.

A durable booth gives you permission to wait.

Pillar 5 — Emotional Separation Between You and the Booth
This is the hardest pillar—and the most important.

Durability requires that the booth is not an extension of your identity.

> If every slow week feels personal, the booth owns you.
> If every comment cuts deep, the booth controls you.
> If every change feels like judgment, the booth drains you.

Durable vendors maintain **emotional distance**.

They care—but they do not attach.

They observe—but they do not spiral.

They respond—but they do not overcorrect.

This distance is only possible when the other four pillars are strong. Structure creates emotional safety. Emotional safety creates longevity.

The Durability Test
If you want to know whether your booth is durable, ask these questions honestly:

- Could I step away for three weeks without anxiety?
- Would my booth still look intentional after several sales?
- Do I trust my pricing without constant review?
- Does my inventory replenish without stress?
- Does the booth support my life—or compete with it?

Durability is not built in a weekend.
But it is built through subtraction, clarity, and restraint.

Durability is not about doing more.

It is about designing something that does not need you at full capacity all the time.

When your booth becomes structurally durable, everything changes:

- your relationship with selling
- your relationship with time
- your relationship with success

And that is what allows vendors not just to survive the market—but to stay long enough to benefit from it.

Chapter Takeaway
This chapter was not about pushing further.
It was about deciding when pushing stops being the answer.

By this point in the book, you already know *how* to run a booth. You understand inventory logic, layout systems, pricing discipline, and customer behavior. What remains is not knowledge—it's judgment.

This chapter asked you to look at your booth differently.

> Not as a project that constantly needs improvement.
> Not as a reflection of your effort or creativity.
> Not as something that must always be in motion to be successful.

But as a system designed to endure.

Durability is the outcome of restraint.

It comes from choosing inventory that replenishes without stress. From layouts that survive disruption instead of collapsing under it.
From pricing systems that reduce decision fatigue instead of creating it.
From maintenance rhythms that replace urgency with intention.

And most importantly, from emotional separation—where your booth matters, but does not define you.

A durable booth does not demand your best energy every week.

It functions when your attention is divided.
It survives when life intervenes.
It remains coherent when enthusiasm dips.

That is not accidental.
It is designed.

This chapter reframed success away from excitement and toward sustainability. It challenged the assumption that growth is always progress and that constant optimization is always responsible. Instead, it introduced a quieter metric:

Can your booth hold without you holding it up?

If the answer is yes, you've built something rare.
If the answer is no, durability—not effort—is what's missing.

Durability does not mean stagnation.
It means optionality.

It gives you the ability to pause without panic.
To observe instead of react.
To change when change is warranted—not when anxiety demands it.

Vendors who last do not win by intensity.
They win by designing systems that remove unnecessary pressure.

If this chapter felt slower, more reflective, or less tactical than others, that was intentional. Durability is not a tactic—it's a posture. It shows up only after you've stopped chasing proof and started protecting what works.

The market will always test you.
Durable booths pass those tests quietly.

They don't impress everyone.
They don't rely on momentum.
They don't burn bright and disappear.

They persist.

And persistence, over time, outperforms everything else.

After the Hustle

There will come a moment—if it hasn't already—when you realize something has changed.

The booth no longer feels heavy.
You stop checking numbers with a knot in your stomach.
A slow week registers as information instead of threat.

Nothing dramatic happens. No announcement. No finish line.

Just quiet confidence.

That's when you know the hustle has done its job.

Hustle is not a failure. It's a phase. It carries you through uncertainty, experimentation, and learning. It teaches you how the market behaves and how *you* behave inside it.

But hustle is not where you live.

What comes after is steadier. Calmer. More deliberate.

You start making fewer decisions—not because you care less, but because the systems you built are doing the work. Your booth begins to hold itself together. You intervene with intention instead of urgency.

This is where selling stops feeling like something you survive and starts feeling like something you maintain.

The market will keep changing. It always will. But you no longer feel the need to chase every shift. You recognize what applies to you and what doesn't. You move when movement matters and stay still when stillness protects what's already working.

That discernment is earned.

Over time, you'll notice another change—one that most vendors never name.

You stop needing proof.

> You don't need every month to be better than the last.
> You don't need constant validation.

You don't need to explain your approach to people who don't understand it.

Your booth doesn't shout.
It doesn't scramble.
It doesn't burn you out to justify its existence.

It works.

And because it works, it gives you something far more valuable than growth: choice.

> **You** can grow if you want to.
> **You** can stay steady if you don't.
> **You** can pivot, simplify, expand, or pause.

None of those options feel like failure anymore.

That's the difference between chasing success and owning it.

If this book has done its job, you don't feel fired up right now.

You feel grounded.

You feel clearer about what belongs in your booth—and what doesn't.
You feel less reactive and more observant.
You feel capable of stepping back without fear.

That's not the absence of ambition.

It's maturity.

The vendors who last aren't the ones who hustle forever.

They're the ones who know when the hustle has served its purpose—and when it's time to build something that lasts.

Set your booth up to hold
Protect your energy
Trust what works
Let the rest go
Keep Hustling

About the Author

Rodney Baker is the owner of Rustique Relics LLC, a multi-vendor antique and boutique marketplace located in Clanton, Alabama. What began as his mother-in-law Margaret's dream has grown into a thriving retail destination that blends vintage charm, handmade creativity, and community pride.

With years of hands-on experience managing vendor spaces, curating inventory, and helping others succeed in the antique mall industry, Rodney now shares the real strategies behind profitable booths. Through Rustique Relics, he and his wife Missy have launched an online store, subscription boxes, and a social media following that continues to grow.

When he's not helping vendors build better booths, you'll find Rodney restoring vintage pieces, working on new product ideas, or encouraging others to turn their passion into a business they're proud of.

www.ingramcontent.com/pod-product-compliance
Lightning Source LLC
Chambersburg PA
CBHW060337200326
41519CB00011BA/1961